# SIMPLE
# HOME BAKING

# SIMPLE
# HOME BAKING

## A WONDERFUL COLLECTION OF IRRESISTIBLE HOME BAKES AND CAKES, WITH 70 CLASSIC RECIPES SHOWN IN 300 STEP-BY-STEP PHOTOGRAPHS

## CAROLE CLEMENTS

HERMES HOUSE

This edition is published by Hermes House, an imprint of Anness Publishing Ltd,
Blaby Road, Wigston, Leicestershire LE18 4SE
Email: info@anness.com
Web: www.hermeshouse.com; www.annesspublishing.com

If you like the images in this book and would like to investigate using them for publishing, promotions
or advertising, please visit our website www.practicalpictures.com for more information.

Main front cover image shows a chocolate chip brownie – for recipe, see page 18.

## ETHICAL TRADING POLICY

At Anness Publishing we believe that business should be conducted in an ethical and ecologically sustainable way,
with respect for the environment and a proper regard to the replacement of the natural resources we employ.
As a publisher, we use a lot of wood pulp to make high-quality paper for printing, and that wood commonly comes
from spruce trees. We are therefore currently growing more than 750,000 trees in three Scottish forest plantations.
These forests contain more than 3.5 times the number of trees used each year in making paper for our books.
Because of this ongoing ecological investment programme, you, as our customer, can have the pleasure and reassurance
of knowing that a tree is being cultivated on your behalf to naturally replace the materials used to make the book you
are holding. For further information about this scheme, go to www.annesspublishing.com/trees

## ACKNOWLEDGEMENTS

For their assistance in the production of this book, the publishers wish to thank the following:
American Country Collections Limited, Weybridge, Surrey; British Gas North Thames, Staines, Middlesex;
Kenwood Appliances plc, Havant, Hampshire; Magimix, Godalming, Surrey; Prestige, Egham, Surrey.

Publisher: Joanna Lorenz
Project Editor: Carole Clements
Copy Editors: Laura Washburn and Elizabeth Wolf-Cohen
Designer: Sheila Volpe
Photographer and Stylist: Amanda Heywood
Food Styling: Elizabeth Wolf-Cohen, Carla Capalbo,
steps by Carla Hobday, Teresa Goldfinch, Nicola Fowler
Typeset by SMI

© Anness Publishing Ltd 1994, 2011

Previously published as *Easy Home Baking*

## NOTES

For all recipes, quantities are given in both metric and imperial measures and, where appropriate, in standard
cups and spoons. Follow one set of measures, but not a mixture, because they are not interchangeable.
Standard spoon and cup measures are level. 1 tsp = 5ml, 1 tbsp = 15ml, 1 cup = 250ml/8fl oz.
Australian standard tablespoons are 20ml. Australian readers should use 3 tsp in place of 1 tbsp for small quantities.
American pints are 16fl oz/2 cups. American readers should use 20fl oz/2$^1/_2$ cups in place of 1 pint when measuring liquids.
Electric oven temperatures in this book are for conventional ovens. When using a fan oven, the temperature will
probably need to be reduced by about 10–20°C/20–40°F. Since ovens vary, you should check
with your manufacturer's instruction book for guidance.
For best results, where a baking tin is specified, use a 3–5 cm (1$^1/_2$–2 in) deep tin.
Medium (US large) eggs are used unless otherwise stated.

## PUBLISHER'S NOTE

Although the advice and information in this book are believed to be accurate and true at the time of going to press,
neither the authors nor the publisher can accept any legal responsibility or liability for any errors or omissions
that may have been made nor for any inaccuracies nor for any loss, harm or injury that comes about
from following instructions or advice in this book.

# Contents

# INTRODUCTION

Nothing equals the satisfaction of home baking. No commercial cake mix or shop-bought biscuit can match one that is made from the best fresh ingredients, with all the added enjoyment that baking at home provides – the enticing aromas that fill the house and stimulate appetites, the delicious straight-from-the-oven flavour, as well as the pride of having created such wonderful goodies yourself.

This book is filled with familiar favourites as well as many other less-well known but equally good recipes. Explore the wealth of biscuits, cookies, buns, tea breads, yeast breads, pies, tarts, and cakes within these pages. Even if you are a novice baker, the easy-to-follow and clear step-by-step photographs will help you achieve good results. For the more experienced home baker, this book will provide some new recipes to add to your repertoire.

Baking is an exact science, and the best results will be achieved by approaching each recipe in a methodical way. First, read through the recipe from beginning to end. Set out all the required ingredients before you begin. Medium eggs are assumed unless specified otherwise, and they should be at room temperature for best results. Sift the flour after you have measured it, and incorporate other dry ingredients as specified in the individual recipes. If you sift the flour from a fair height, it will have more chance to aerate and lighten.

When a recipe calls for folding one ingredient into another, it should be done in a way that incorporates as much air as possible into the mixture. Use either a large metal spoon or a long rubber or plastic scraper. Gently plunge the spoon or scraper deep into the centre of the mixture and, scooping up a large amount of the mixture, fold it over. Turn the bowl slightly so each scoop folds over another part of the mixture.

No two ovens are alike. Buy a reliable oven thermometer and test the temperature of your oven. When possible, bake in the centre of the oven where the heat is more likely to be constant. If using a fan-assisted oven, follow the manufacturer's guidelines for baking. Good quality baking tins can improve your results, as they conduct heat more efficiently.

Finally, practice, patience and enthusiasm are the keys to confident and successful baking. The recipes that follow will inspire you to start sifting flour, breaking eggs and stirring up all sorts of delectable home-made treats – all guaranteed to bring great satisfaction to both the baker and those lucky enough to enjoy the results.

# Biscuits & Bars

Keep the biscuit tin filled with this wonderful array of biscuits
and bars – some soft and chewy, some crunchy and nutty,
some rich and sinful, and some plain and wholesome.
All are irresistible.

# Nut Lace Wafers

**MAKES 18**

| |
|---|
| 2½ oz (70 g) whole blanched almonds |
| 2 oz (55 g) butter |
| 1½ oz (45 g) plain flour |
| 3½ oz (100 g) sugar |
| 1 fl oz (30 ml) double cream |
| ½ teaspoon vanilla essence |

**1** Preheat the oven to 375°F/190°C/Gas 5. Grease 1–2 baking sheets.

**2** With a sharp knife, chop the almonds as fine as possible. Alternatively, use a food processor, blender, or coffee grinder to chop the nuts very fine.

**3** ▼ Melt the butter in a saucepan over low heat. Remove from the heat and stir in the remaining ingredients and the almonds.

**4** Drop teaspoonfuls 2½ in (6 cm) apart on the prepared sheets. Bake until golden, about 5 minutes. Cool on the baking sheets briefly, just until the wafers are stiff enough to remove.

**5** ▲ With a metal palette knife, transfer to a rack to cool completely.

> **~ VARIATION ~**
>
> Add 2 oz (55 g) finely chopped orange peel to the mixture.

---

# Oatmeal Lace Rounds

**MAKES 36**

| |
|---|
| 5½ oz (150 g) butter or margarine |
| 4½ oz (125 g) quick-cooking porridge oats |
| 5¾ oz (165 g) dark brown sugar |
| 5¼ oz (150 g) caster sugar |
| 1½ oz (45 g) plain flour |
| ¼ teaspoon salt |
| 1 egg, lightly beaten |
| 1 teaspoon vanilla essence |
| 2½ oz (70 g) pecans or walnuts, finely chopped |

**1** Preheat the oven to 350°F/180°C/Gas 4. Grease 2 baking sheets.

**2** Melt the butter in a saucepan over low heat. Set aside.

**3** In a mixing bowl, combine the oats, brown sugar, caster sugar, flour and salt.

**4** ▲ Make a well in the centre and add the butter or margarine, egg and vanilla.

**5** ▼ Mix until blended, then stir in the chopped nuts.

**6** Drop rounded teaspoonfuls of the mixture about 2 in (5 cm) apart on the prepared sheets. Bake until lightly browned on the edges and bubbling, 5–8 minutes. Let cool on the sheet for 2 minutes, then transfer to a rack to cool completely.

*Nut Lace Wafers (top), Oatmeal Lace Rounds*

# Italian Almond Biscotti

**MAKES 48**

| |
|---|
| 7 oz (200 g) whole unblanched almonds |
| 7¹/₂ oz (215 g) plain flour |
| 3¹/₂ oz (100 g) sugar |
| ¹/₈ teaspoon salt |
| ¹/₈ teaspoon saffron powder |
| ¹/₂ teaspoon bicarbonate of soda |
| 2 eggs |
| 1 egg white, lightly beaten |

---

**~ COOK'S TIP ~**

Serve biscotti after a meal,
for dunking in glasses of sweet
white wine, such as an Italian
*Vin Santo* or a French *Muscat de
Beaumes-de-Venise.*

---

1 Preheat a 375°F/190°C/Gas 5 oven.
Grease and flour 2 baking sheets.

2 ▲ Spread the almonds in a baking
tray and bake until lightly browned,
about 15 minutes. When cool, grind
2 oz (55 g) of the almonds in a food
processor, blender, or coffee grinder
until pulverized. Coarsely chop the
remaining almonds in 2 or 3 pieces
each. Set aside.

3 ▲ Combine the flour, sugar, salt,
saffron, bicarbonate of soda and
ground almonds in a bowl and mix to
blend. Make a well in the centre and
add the eggs. Stir to form a rough
dough. Transfer to a floured surface
and knead until well blended. Knead
in the chopped almonds.

4 ▲ Divide the dough into 3 equal
parts. Roll into logs about 1 in (2.5
cm) in diameter. Place on one of the
prepared sheets, brush with the egg
white and bake for 20 minutes.
Remove from the oven.

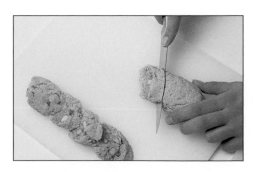

5 ▲ With a very sharp knife, cut
into each log at an angle making ¹/₂ in
(1 cm) slices. Return the slices on the
baking sheets to a 275°F/140°C/ Gas 1
oven and bake for 25 minutes more.
Transfer to a rack to cool.

# Orange Biscuits

**MAKES 30**

| |
|---|
| 4 oz (115 g) butter, at room temperature |
| 7 oz (200 g) sugar |
| 2 egg yolks |
| 1 tablespoon fresh orange juice |
| grated rind of 1 large orange |
| 7 oz (200 g) plain flour |
| 1 tablespoon cornflour |
| $^1/_2$ teaspoon salt |
| 1 teaspoon baking powder |

**1** ▲ With an electric mixer, cream the butter and sugar until light and fluffy. Add the yolks, orange juice and rind, and continue beating to blend. Set aside.

**2** In another bowl, sift together the flour, cornflour, salt and baking powder. Add to the butter mixture and stir until it forms a dough.

**3** ▲ Wrap the dough in greaseproof paper and refrigerate for 2 hours.

**4** Preheat the oven to 375°F/190°C/ Gas 5. Grease 2 baking sheets.

**5** ▲ Roll spoonfuls of the dough into balls and place 1–2 in (2.5–5 cm) apart on the prepared sheets.

**6** ▼ Press down with a fork to flatten. Bake until golden brown, 8–10 minutes. With a metal palette knife transfer to a rack to cool.

# Peanut Butter Biscuits

**MAKES 24**

5 oz (140 g) plain flour

1/2 teaspoon bicarbonate of soda

1/2 teaspoon salt

4 oz (115 g) butter, at room temperature

5³/4 oz (165 g) light brown sugar

1 egg

1 teaspoon vanilla essence

9¹/2 oz (265 g) crunchy peanut butter

**1** Sift together the flour, bicarbonate of soda and salt and set aside.

**2** With an electric mixer, cream the butter and sugar together until light and fluffy.

**3** In another bowl, mix the egg and vanilla, then gradually beat into the butter mixture.

**4** ▲ Stir in the peanut butter and blend thoroughly. Stir in the dry ingredients. Refrigerate for at least 30 minutes, or until firm.

**5** Preheat the oven to 350°F/180°C/ Gas 4. Grease 2 baking sheets.

**6** Spoon out rounded teaspoonfuls of the dough and roll into balls.

**7** ▲ Place the balls on the prepared sheets and press flat with a fork into circles about 2¹/2 in (6 cm) in diameter, making a criss-cross pattern. Bake until lightly coloured, 12–15 minutes. Transfer to a rack to cool.

---

**~ VARIATION ~**

Add 3 oz (85 g) peanuts, coarsely chopped, with the peanut butter.

---

# Chocolate Chip Cookies

**MAKES 24**

4 oz (115 g) butter or margarine, at room temperature

1³/4 oz (50 g) caster sugar

3³/4 oz (110 g) dark brown sugar

1 egg

1/2 teaspoon vanilla essence

6 oz (170 g) plain flour

1/2 teaspoon bicarbonate of soda

1/8 teaspoon salt

6 oz (170 g) chocolate chips

2 oz (55 g) walnuts, chopped

**1** Preheat the oven to 350°F/180°C/ Gas 4. Grease 2 large baking sheets.

**2** ▼ With an electric mixer, cream the butter or margarine and two sugars together until light and fluffy.

**3** In another bowl, mix the egg and vanilla, then gradually beat into the butter mixture. Sift over the flour, bicarbonate of soda and salt and stir.

**4** ▲ Add the chocolate chips and walnuts, and mix to combine well.

**5** Place heaped teaspoonfuls of the dough 2 in (5 cm) apart on the prepared sheets. Bake until lightly coloured, 10–15 minutes. Transfer to a rack to cool.

*Peanut Butter Biscuits (top), Chocolate Chip Cookies*

# Chocolate Pretzels

**MAKES 28**

| |
| --- |
| 5 oz (140 g) plain flour |
| 1/8 teaspoon salt |
| 3/4 oz (25 g) unsweetened cocoa powder |
| 4 oz (115 g) butter, at room temperature |
| 4 1/2 oz (125 g) sugar |
| 1 egg |
| 1 egg white, lightly beaten, for glazing |
| sugar crystals, for sprinkling |

**1** Sift together the flour, salt and cocoa powder. Set aside. Grease 2 baking sheets.

**2 ▲** With an electric mixer, cream the butter until light. Add the sugar and continue beating until light and fluffy. Beat in the egg. Add the dry ingredients and stir to blend. Gather the dough into a ball, wrap in clear film, and refrigerate for 1 hour or freeze for 30 minutes.

**3 ▲** Roll the dough into 28 small balls. Refrigerate the balls until needed. Preheat the oven to 375°F/190°C/Gas 5.

**4 ▲** Roll each ball into a rope about 10 in (25 cm) long. With each rope, form a loop with the two ends facing you. Twist the ends and fold back on to the circle, pressing in to make a pretzel shape. Place on the sheets.

**5 ▲** Brush the pretzels with the egg white. Sprinkle sugar crystals over the tops and bake until firm, 10–12 minutes. Transfer to a rack to cool.

# Florentines

**MAKES 36**

| |
|---|
| 1½ oz (45 g) butter |
| 4 fl oz (125 ml) whipping cream |
| 4½ oz (125 g) sugar |
| 4½ oz (125 g) flaked almonds |
| 2 oz (55 g) orange or mixed peel, finely chopped |
| 1½ oz (45 g) glacé cherries, chopped |
| 2½ oz (70 g) plain flour, sifted |
| 8 oz (225 g) plain chocolate |
| 1 teaspoon vegetable oil |

**1** Preheat the oven to 350°F/180°C/ Gas 4. Grease 2 baking sheets.

**2** ▲ Melt the butter, cream and sugar together and slowly bring to the boil. Take off the heat and stir in the almonds, orange or mixed peel, cherries and flour until blended.

**3** Drop teaspoonfuls of the batter 1–2 in (2.5–5 cm) apart on the prepared sheets and flatten them using a fork.

**4** Bake until the cookies brown at the edges, about 10 minutes. Remove from the oven and correct the shape by quickly pushing in any thin uneven edges with a knife or a round biscuit cutter. Work fast or they will cool and harden while still on the sheets. If necessary, return to the oven for a few moments to soften. While still hot, use a metal palette knife to transfer the florentines to a clean, flat surface.

**5** Melt the chocolate in the top of a double boiler or in a heatproof bowl set over a pan of hot water. Add the oil and stir to blend.

**6** ▲ With a metal palette knife, spread the smooth underside of the cooled florentines with a thin coating of the melted chocolate.

**7** ▼ When the chocolate is about to set, draw a serrated knife across the surface with a slight sawing motion to make wavy lines. Store in an airtight container in a cool place.

# Shortbread

## MAKES 8

5½ oz (150 g) unsalted butter, at room temperature

3½ oz (100 g) caster sugar

6¼ oz (180 g) plain flour

2 oz (55 g) rice flour

¼ teaspoon baking powder

⅛ teaspoon salt

1 Preheat the oven to 325°F/170°C/Gas 3. Grease a shallow 8 in (20 cm) cake tin, preferably with a removable bottom.

2 With an electric mixer, cream the butter and sugar together until light and fluffy. Sift over the flours, baking powder and salt and mix well.

3 ▲ Press the dough neatly into the prepared tin, smoothing the surface with the back of a spoon.

4 Prick all over with a fork, then score into 8 equal wedges.

5 ▲ Bake until golden, 40–45 minutes. Leave in the tin until cool enough to handle, then turn out and recut the wedges while still hot. Store in an airtight container.

# Flapjacks

## MAKES 8

2 oz (55 g) butter

1 rounded tablespoon golden syrup

2¾ oz (80 g) dark brown sugar

3½ oz (100 g) quick-cooking porridge oats

⅛ teaspoon salt

1 ▲ Preheat a 350°F/180°C/Gas 4 oven. Line an 8 in (20 cm) cake tin with greaseproof paper and grease.

2 ▼ Place the butter, golden syrup and sugar in a saucepan over a low heat. Cook, stirring, until melted and combined.

~ VARIATION ~

If wished, add 1 teaspoon ground ginger to the melted butter.

3 ▲ Remove from the heat and add the oats and salt. Stir to blend.

4 Spoon into the prepared tin and smooth the surface. Place in the centre of the oven and bake until golden brown, 20–25 minutes. Leave in the tin until cool enough to handle, then turn out and cut into wedges while still hot.

*Shortbread (top), Flapjacks*

# Chocolate Chip Brownies

**MAKES 24**

4 oz (115 g) plain chocolate

4 oz (115 g) butter

3 eggs

7 oz (200 g) sugar

1/2 teaspoon vanilla essence

pinch of salt

5 oz (140 g) plain flour

6 oz (170 g) chocolate chips

**1 ▼** Preheat a 350°F/180°C/Gas 4 oven. Line a 13 × 9 in (33 × 23 cm) tin with greaseproof paper and grease.

**2 ▲** Melt the chocolate and butter in the top of a double boiler, or in a heatproof bowl set over a pan of gently simmering water.

**3 ▲** Beat together the eggs, sugar, vanilla and salt. Stir in the chocolate mixture. Sift over the flour and fold in. Add the chocolate chips.

**4 ▲** Pour the mixture into the prepared tin and spread evenly. Bake until just set, about 30 minutes. Do not overbake; the brownies should be slightly moist inside. Cool in the pan.

**5** To turn out, run a knife all around the edge and invert onto a baking sheet. Remove the paper. Place another sheet on top and invert again so the brownies are right-side up. Cut into squares for serving.

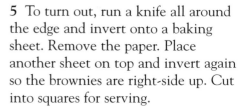

# Marbled Brownies

**MAKES 24**

8 oz (225 g) plain chocolate

3 oz (85 g) butter

4 eggs

10½ oz (300 g) sugar

5 oz (140 g) plain flour

½ teaspoon salt

1 teaspoon baking powder

2 teaspoons vanilla essence

4 oz (115 g) walnuts, chopped

FOR THE PLAIN MIXTURE

2 oz (55 g) butter, at room temperature

6 oz (170 g) cream cheese

3½ oz (100 g) sugar

2 eggs

1 oz (30 g) plain flour

1 teaspoon vanilla essence

**1** Preheat a 350°F/180°C/Gas 4 oven. Line a 13 × 9 in (33 × 23 cm) tin with greaseproof paper and grease.

**2** Melt the chocolate and butter over very low heat, stirring constantly. Set aside to cool.

**3** Meanwhile, beat the eggs until light and fluffy. Gradually add the sugar and continue beating until blended. Sift over the flour, salt and baking powder and fold to combine.

**4** ▲ Stir in the cooled chocolate mixture. Add the vanilla and walnuts. Measure and set aside 16 fl oz (450 ml) of the chocolate mixture.

**5** ▲ For the plain mixture, cream the butter and cream cheese with an electric mixer.

**6** Add the sugar and continue beating until blended. Beat in the eggs, flour and vanilla.

**7** Spread the unmeasured chocolate mixture in the tin. Pour over the plain mixture. Drop spoonfuls of the reserved chocolate mixture on top.

**8** ▲ With a metal palette knife, swirl the mixtures to marble. Do not blend completely. Bake until just set, 35–40 minutes. Turn out when cool and cut into squares for serving.

# Spiced Raisin Bars

**MAKES 30**

3¾ oz (110 g) plain flour

1½ teaspoons baking powder

1 teaspoon ground cinnamon

½ teaspoon grated nutmeg

¼ teaspoon ground cloves

¼ teaspoon ground allspsice

7½ oz (215 g) raisins

4 oz (115 g) butter or margarine, at room temperature

3½ oz (100 g) sugar

2 eggs

5¾ oz (165 g) molasses

2 oz (55 g) walnuts, chopped

**1** Preheat a 350°F/180°C/Gas 4 oven. Line a 13 × 9 in (33 × 23 cm) tin with greaseproof paper and grease.

**2** Sift together the flour, baking powder and spices.

**3** ▲ Place the raisins in another bowl and toss with a few tablespoons of the flour mixture.

**4** ▲ With an electric mixer, cream the butter or margarine and sugar together until light and fluffy. Beat in the eggs, 1 at a time, then the molasses. Stir in the flour mixture, raisins and walnuts.

**5** Spread evenly in the tin. Bake until just set, 15–18 minutes. Let cool in the tin before cutting into bars.

---

# Toffee Meringue Bars

**MAKES 12**

2 oz (55 g) butter

7½ oz (215 g) dark brown sugar

1 egg

½ teaspoon vanilla essence

2½ oz (70 g) plain flour

½ teaspoon salt

¼ teaspoon grated nutmeg

FOR THE TOPPING

1 egg white

⅛ teaspoon salt

1 tablespoon golden syrup

3½ oz (100 g) caster sugar

2 oz (55 g) walnuts, finely chopped

**1** ▲ Combine the butter and brown sugar in a saucepan and heat until bubbling. Set aside to cool.

**2** Preheat the oven to 350°F/180°C/ Gas 4. Line the bottom and sides of an 8 in (20 cm) square cake tin with greaseproof paper and grease.

**3** Beat the egg and vanilla into cooled sugar mixture. Sift over the flour, salt and nutmeg and fold in. Spread in the bottom of the tin.

**4** ▲ For the topping, beat the egg white with the salt until it holds soft peaks. Beat in the golden syrup, then the sugar and continue beating until the mixture holds stiff peaks. Fold in the nuts and spread on top. Bake for 30 minutes. Cut into bars when cool.

*Spiced Raisin Bars (top), Toffee Meringue Bars*

# Chocolate Walnut Bars

**MAKES 24**

| |
|---|
| 2 oz (55 g) walnuts |
| 2¼ oz (60 g) caster sugar |
| 3¾ oz (110 g) plain flour, sifted |
| 3 oz (85 g) cold unsalted butter, cut into pieces |
| FOR THE TOPPING |
| 1 oz (30 g) unsalted butter |
| 3 fl oz (85 ml) water |
| 1 oz (30 g) unsweetened cocoa powder |
| 3½ oz (100 g) caster sugar |
| 1 teaspoon vanilla essence |
| ⅛ teaspoon salt |
| 2 eggs |
| icing sugar, for dusting |

**1** Preheat a 350°F/180°C/Gas 4 oven. Grease the bottom and sides of an 8 in (20 cm) square baking tin.

**2** ▼ Grind the walnuts with a few tablespoons of the sugar in a food processor, blender or coffee grinder.

**3** In a bowl, combine the ground walnuts, remaining sugar and flour. With your fingertips, rub in the butter until the mixture resembles coarse breadcrumbs. Alternatively, process all the ingredients in a food processor until the mixture resembles coarse breadcrumbs.

**4** ▲ Pat the walnut mixture into the bottom of the prepared tin in an even layer. Bake for 25 minutes.

**5** ▲ Meanwhile, for the topping, melt the butter with the water. Whisk in the cocoa and sugar. Remove from the heat, stir in the vanilla and salt and let cool for 5 minutes. Whisk in the eggs until blended.

**6** ▲ Pour the topping over the crust when baked.

**7** Return to the oven and bake until set, about 20 minutes. Set the tin on a rack to cool. Cut into 2½ × 1 in (6 × 2.5 cm) bars and dust with icing sugar. Store in the refrigerator.

# Muffins & Tea Breads

Easy to make and satisfying to eat, these muffins and tea breads will fill the house with the aroma of baking and lure your family and friends to linger over breakfast, coffee or tea – and they are great for snacks or lunch, too.

# Chocolate Chip Muffins

**MAKES 10**

4 oz (115 g) butter or margarine, at room
temperature

2¹/₂ oz (70 g) caster sugar

1 oz (30 g) dark brown sugar

2 eggs, at room temperature

7¹/₂ oz (215 g) plain flour

1 teaspoon baking powder

4 fl oz (125 ml) milk

6 oz (170 g) plain chocolate chips

1   Preheat the oven to 375°F/190°C/
Gas 5. Grease 10 muffin cups or use
paper cases.

2 ▼   With an electric mixer, cream
the butter until soft. Add both sugars
and beat until light and fluffy. Beat in
the eggs, 1 at a time.

3   Sift together the flour and baking
powder, twice. Fold into the butter
mixture, alternating with the milk.

4 ▲   Divide half the mixture between
the muffin cups. Sprinkle several
chocolate chips on top, then cover
with a spoonful of the batter. To
ensure even baking, half-fill any
empty cups with water.

5   Bake until lightly coloured, about
25 minutes. Let stand 5 minutes
before turning out.

# Chocolate Walnut Muffins

**MAKES 12**

6 oz (170 g) unsalted butter

5 oz (140 g) plain chocolate

7 oz (200 g) caster sugar

2 oz (55 g) dark brown sugar

4 eggs

1 teaspoon vanilla essence

¹/₄ teaspoon almond essence

3³/₄ oz (110 g) plain flour

1 tablespoon unsweetened cocoa powder

4 oz (115 g) walnuts, chopped

1   Preheat the oven to 350°F/180°C/
Gas 4. Grease a 12-cup muffin pan or
use paper cases.

2 ▼   Melt the butter with the
chocolate in the top of a double boiler
or in a heatproof bowl set over a pan
of hot water. Transfer to a large
mixing bowl.

3   Stir both the sugars into the
chocolate mixture. Mix in the eggs,
1 at a time, then add the vanilla and
almond essences.

4   Sift over the flour and cocoa.

5 ▲   Fold in and stir in the walnuts.

6   Fill the prepared cups almost to the
top and bake until a skewer inserted in
the centre barely comes out clean,
30–35 minutes. Let stand 5 minutes
before turning out onto a rack to cool
completely.

*Chocolate Chip Muffins (top), Chocolate Walnut Muffins*

# Prune Muffins

**MAKES 12**

1 egg

8 fl oz (250 ml) milk

4 fl oz (125 ml) vegetable oil

1 ¾ oz (50 g) caster sugar

1 oz (30 g) dark brown sugar

10 oz (285 g) plain flour

2 teaspoons baking powder

½ teaspoon salt

¼ teaspoon grated nutmeg

4 oz (115 g) cooked stoned prunes,
  chopped

1  Preheat a 400°F/200°C/Gas 6 oven. Grease a 12-cup muffin tin.

2  Break the egg into a mixing bowl and beat with a fork. Beat in the milk and oil.

3 ▼  Stir in the sugars. Set aside.

4  Sift the flour, baking powder, salt and nutmeg into a mixing bowl. Make a well in the centre, pour in the egg mixture and stir until moistened. Do not overmix; the batter should be slightly lumpy.

5 ▲  Fold in the prunes.

6  Fill the prepared cups two-thirds full. Bake until golden brown, about 20 minutes. Let stand 10 minutes before turning out. Serve warm or at room temperature.

# Yogurt and Honey Muffins

**MAKES 12**

2 oz (55 g) butter

5 tablespoons clear honey

8 fl oz (250 ml) plain yogurt

1 large egg, at room temperature

grated rind of 1 lemon

2 fl oz (65 ml) lemon juice

5 oz (140 g) plain flour

6 oz (170 g) wholemeal flour

1½ teaspoons bicarbonate of soda

⅛ teaspoon grated nutmeg

~ VARIATION ~

For Walnut Yogurt Honey Muffins, add 2 oz (55 g) chopped walnuts, folded in with the flour. This makes a more substantial muffin.

1  Preheat a 375°F/190°C/Gas 5 oven. Grease a 12-cup muffin tin or use paper cases.

2  In a saucepan, melt the butter and honey. Remove from the heat and set aside to cool slightly.

3 ▲  In a bowl, whisk together the yogurt, egg, lemon rind and juice. Add the butter and honey mixture. Set aside.

4 ▲  In another bowl, sift together the dry ingredients.

5  Fold the dry ingredients into the yogurt mixture to blend.

6  Fill the prepared cups two-thirds full. Bake until the tops spring back when touched lightly, 20–25 minutes. Let cool in the tin for 5 minutes before turning out. Serve warm or at room temperature.

*Prune Muffins (top), Yogurt and Honey Muffins*

# Blueberry Muffins

**MAKES 12**

6¼ oz (180 g) plain flour

2¼ oz (60 g) sugar

2 teaspoons baking powder

¼ teaspoon salt

2 eggs

2 oz (55 g) butter, melted

6 fl oz (175 ml) milk

1 teaspoon vanilla essence

1 teaspoon grated lemon rind

6 oz (170 g) fresh blueberries

**1**   Preheat a 400°F/200°C/Gas 6 oven.

**2** ▼   Grease a 12-cup muffin tin or use paper cases.

**3** ▲   Sift the flour, sugar, baking powder and salt into a bowl.

**4**   In another bowl, whisk the eggs until blended. Add the melted butter, milk, vanilla and lemon rind and stir to combine.

**5**   Make a well in the dry ingredients and pour in the egg mixture. With a large metal spoon, stir just until the flour is moistened, not until smooth.

**6** ▲   Fold in the blueberries.

**7** ▲   Spoon the batter into the cups, leaving room for the muffins to rise.

**8**   Bake until the tops spring back when touched lightly, 20–25 minutes. Let cool in the pan for 5 minutes before turning out.

# Apple and Cranberry Muffins

**MAKES 12**

| |
|---|
| 2 oz (55 g) butter or margarine |
| 1 egg |
| 3½ oz (100 g) sugar |
| grated rind of 1 large orange |
| 4 fl oz (125 ml) freshly squeezed orange juice |
| 5 oz (140 g) plain flour |
| 1 teaspoon baking powder |
| ½ teaspoon bicarbonate of soda |
| 1 teaspoon ground cinnamon |
| ½ teaspoon grated nutmeg |
| ½ teaspoon ground allspice |
| ¼ teaspoon ground ginger |
| ¼ teaspoon salt |
| 1–2 dessert apples |
| 6 oz (170 g) cranberries |
| 2 oz (55 g) walnuts, chopped |
| icing sugar, for dusting (optional) |

**1**   Preheat the oven to 350°F/180°C/ Gas 4. Grease a 12-cup muffin tin or use paper cases.

**2**   Melt the butter or margarine over gentle heat. Set aside to cool.

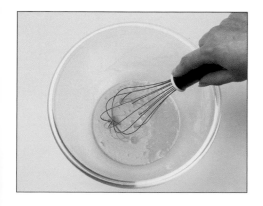

**3** ▲   Place the egg in a mixing bowl and whisk lightly. Add the melted butter or margarine and whisk to combine.

**4**   Add the sugar, orange rind and juice. Whisk to blend, then set aside.

**5**   In a large bowl, sift together the flour, baking powder, bicarbonate of soda, cinnamon, nutmeg, allspice, ginger and salt. Set aside.

**6** ▲   Quarter, core and peel the apples. With a sharp knife, chop coarsely.

**7**   Make a well in the dry ingredients and pour in the egg mixture. With a spoon, stir until just blended.

**8** ▲   Add the apples, cranberries and walnuts and stir to blend.

**9**   Fill the cups three-quarters full and bake until the tops spring back when touched lightly, 25–30 minutes. Transfer to a rack to cool. Dust with icing sugar, if desired.

# Wholemeal Scones

**MAKES 16**

6 oz (170 g) cold butter

12 oz (350 g) wholemeal flour

5 oz (140 g) plain flour

2 tablespoons sugar

$^1/_2$ teaspoon salt

$2^1/_2$ teaspoons bicarbonate of soda

2 eggs

6 fl oz (175 ml) buttermilk

$1^1/_4$ oz (35 g) raisins

1   Preheat the oven to 400°F/ 200°C/Gas 6. Grease and flour a large baking sheet.

2 ▲   Cut the butter into small pieces.

3   Combine the dry ingredients in a bowl. Add the butter and rub it in with your fingertips until the mixture resembles coarse breadcrumbs. Set aside.

4   In another bowl, whisk together the eggs and buttermilk. Set aside 2 tablespoons for glazing.

5   Stir the remaining egg mixture into the dry ingredients until it just holds together. Stir in the raisins.

6   Roll out the dough about $^3/_4$ in (2 cm) thick. Stamp out circles with a biscuit cutter. Place on the prepared sheet and brush with the glaze.

7   Bake until golden, 12–15 minutes. Allow to cool slightly before serving. Split in two with a fork while still warm and spread with butter and jam, if wished.

# Orange and Raisin Scones

**MAKES 16**

10 oz (285 g) plain flour

$1^1/_2$ tablespoons baking powder

$2^1/_4$ oz (60 g) sugar

$^1/_2$ teaspoon salt

$2^1/_2$ g (70 g) butter, diced

$2^1/_2$ g (70 g) margarine, diced

grated rind of 1 large orange

2 oz (55 g) raisins

4 fl oz (125 ml) buttermilk

milk, for glazing

1   Preheat the oven to 425°F/ 220°C/Gas 7. Grease and flour a large baking sheet.

2   Combine the dry ingredients in a large bowl. Add the butter and margarine and rub in with your fingertips until the mixture resembles coarse breadcrumbs.

3 ▲   Add the orange rind and raisins.

4   Gradually stir in the buttermilk to form a soft dough.

5 ▲   Roll out the dough about $^3/_4$ in (2 cm) thick. Stamp out circles with a biscuit cutter.

6 ▲   Place on the prepared sheet and brush the tops with milk.

7   Bake until golden, 12–15 minutes. Serve hot or warm, with butter, or whipped or clotted cream, and jam.

~ COOK'S TIP ~

For light tender scones, handle the dough as little as possible. If you wish, split the scones when cool and toast them under a preheated grill. Butter them while still hot.

*Wholemeal Scones (top), Orange and Raisin Scones*

# Orange and Honey Tea Bread

**MAKES 1 LOAF**

13½ oz (385 g) plain flour

2½ teaspoons baking powder

½ teaspoon bicarbonate of soda

½ teaspoon salt

1 oz (30 g) margarine

8 fl oz (250 ml) clear honey

1 egg, at room temperature, lightly beaten

1½ tablespoons grated orange rind

6 fl oz (175 ml) freshly squeezed orange juice

4 oz (115 g) walnuts, chopped

**1** Preheat a 325°F/170°C/Gas 3 oven.

**2** Sift together the flour, baking powder, bicarbonate of soda and salt.

**3** Line the bottom and sides of a 9 × 5 in (23 × 13 cm) loaf tin with greaseproof paper and grease.

**4** ▲ With an electric mixer, cream the margarine until soft. Stir in the honey until blended, then stir in the egg. Add the orange rind and stir to combine thoroughly.

**5** ▲ Fold the flour mixture into the honey and egg mixture in 3 batches, alternating with the orange juice. Stir in the walnuts.

**6** Pour into the tin and bake until a skewer inserted in the centre comes out clean, 60–70 minutes. Let stand 10 minutes before turning out onto a rack to cool.

# Apple Loaf

**MAKES 1 LOAF**

1 egg

8 fl oz (250 ml) bottled or homemade apple sauce

2 oz (55 g) butter or margarine, melted

3¾ oz (110 g) dark brown sugar

1¾ oz (50 g) caster sugar

10 oz (285 g) plain flour

2 teaspoons baking powder

½ teaspoon bicarbonate of soda

½ teaspoon salt

1 teaspoon ground cinnamon

½ teaspoon grated nutmeg

2½ oz (70 g) currants or raisins

2 oz (55 g) pecans or walnuts, chopped

**1** Preheat a 350°F/180°C/Gas 4 oven. Line a 9 × 5 in (23 × 13 cm) loaf tin with greaseproof paper and grease.

**2** ▲ Break the egg into a bowl and beat lightly. Stir in the apple sauce, butter or margarine and both sugars. Set aside.

**3** In another bowl, sift together the flour, baking powder, bicarbonate of soda, salt, cinnamon and nutmeg. Fold dry ingredients into the apple sauce mixture in 3 batches.

**4** ▼ Stir in the currants or raisins, and nuts.

**5** Pour into the prepared tin and bake until a skewer inserted in the centre comes out clean, about 1 hour. Let stand 10 minutes. Turn out onto a rack and cool completely.

*Orange and Honey Tea Bread (top), Apple Loaf*

# Mango Tea Bread

**MAKES 2 LOAVES**

| |
|---|
| 10 oz (285 g) plain flour |
| 2 teaspoons bicarbonate of soda |
| 2 teaspoons ground cinnamon |
| 1/2 teaspoon salt |
| 4 oz (115 g) margarine, at room temperature |
| 3 eggs, at room temperature |
| 10 1/2 oz (300 g) sugar |
| 4 fl oz (125 ml) vegetable oil |
| 1 large ripe mango, peeled and chopped |
| 3 1/4 oz (90 g) desiccated coconut |
| 2 1/2 oz (70 g) raisins |

**1** Preheat the oven to 350°F/180°C/Gas 4. Line the bottom and sides of 2 9 × 5 in (23 × 13 cm) loaf tins with greaseproof paper and grease.

**2** Sift together the flour, bicarbonate of soda, cinnamon and salt. Set aside.

**3** With an electric mixer, cream the margarine until soft.

**4** ▼ Beat in the eggs and sugar until light and fluffy. Beat in the oil.

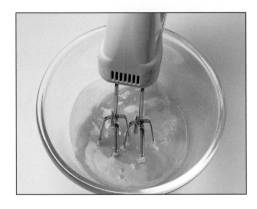

**5** Fold the dry ingredients into the creamed ingredients in 3 batches.

**6** Fold in the mangoes, two-thirds of the coconut and the raisins.

**7** ▲ Spoon the batter into the pans.

**8** Sprinkle over the remaining coconut. Bake until a skewer inserted in the centre comes out clean, 50–60 minutes. Let stand for 10 minutes before turning out onto a rack to cool completely.

# Courgette Tea Bread

**MAKES 1 LOAF**

| |
|---|
| 2 oz (55 g) butter |
| 3 eggs |
| 8 fl oz (250 ml) vegetable oil |
| 10 1/2 oz (300 g) sugar |
| 2 medium unpeeled courgettes, grated |
| 10 oz (285 g) plain flour |
| 2 teaspoons bicarbonate of soda |
| 1 teaspoon baking powder |
| 1 teaspoon salt |
| 1 teaspoon ground cinnamon |
| 1 teaspoon grated nutmeg |
| 1/4 teaspoon ground cloves |
| 4 oz (115 g) walnuts, chopped |

**1** Preheat the oven to 350°F/180°C/Gas 4.

**2** Line the bottom and sides of a 9 × 5 in (23 × 13 cm) loaf tin with greaseproof paper and grease.

**3** ▲ In a saucepan, melt the butter over low heat. Set aside.

**4** With an electric mixer, beat the eggs and oil together until thick. Beat in the sugar. Stir in the melted butter and courgettes. Set aside.

**5** ▲ In another bowl, sift all the dry ingredients together 3 times. Carefully fold into the courgette mixture. Fold in the walnuts.

**6** Pour into the tin and bake until a skewer inserted in the centre comes out clean, 60–70 minutes. Let stand 10 minutes before turning out onto wire rack to cool completely.

*Mango Tea Bread (top), Courgette Tea Bread*

# Glazed Banana Spice Loaf

**MAKES 1 LOAF**

1 large ripe banana

4 oz (115 g) butter, at room temperature

5$^{1}/_{2}$ oz (150 g) caster sugar

2 eggs, at room temperature

7$^{1}/_{2}$ oz (215 g) plain flour

1 teaspoon salt

1 teaspoon bicarbonate of soda

$^{1}/_{2}$ teaspoon grated nutmeg

$^{1}/_{4}$ teaspoon ground allspice

$^{1}/_{4}$ teaspoon ground cloves

6 fl oz (175 ml) soured cream

1 teaspoon vanilla essence

**FOR THE GLAZE**

4 oz (115 g) icing sugar

1–2 tablespoons lemon juice

**1**   Preheat a 350°F/180°C/Gas 4 oven. Line an 8$^{1}/_{2}$ × 4$^{1}/_{2}$ in (21.5 × 11.5 cm) loaf tin with greaseproof and grease.

**2** ▼   With a fork, mash the banana in a bowl. Set aside.

**3**   With an electric mixer, cream the butter and sugar until light and fluffy. Add the eggs, 1 at a time, beating to blend well after each addition.

**4**   Sift together the flour, salt, bicarbonate of soda, nutmeg, allspice and cloves. Add to the butter mixture and stir to combine well.

**5** ▲   Add the soured cream, banana, and vanilla and mix just enough to blend. Pour into the prepared tin.

**6** ▲   Bake until the top springs back when touched lightly, 45–50 minutes. Let cool in the pan for 10 minutes. Turn out onto a wire rack to cool.

**7** ▲   For the glaze, combine the icing sugar and lemon juice, then stir until smooth.

**8**   To glaze, place the cooled loaf on a rack set over a baking sheet. Pour the glaze over the top of the loaf and allow to set.

# Sweet Sesame Loaf

### MAKES 1 OR 2 LOAVES

| |
|---|
| 3 oz (85 g) sesame seeds |
| 10 oz (285 g) plain flour |
| 2½ teaspoons baking powder |
| 1 teaspoon salt |
| 2 oz (55 g) butter or margarine, at room temperature |
| 4½ oz (125 g) sugar |
| 2 eggs, at room temperature |
| grated rind of 1 lemon |
| 12 fl oz (350 ml) milk |

**1** Preheat a 350°F/180°C/Gas 4 oven. Line a 9 × 5 in (23 × 13 cm) loaf tin with greaseproof paper and grease.

**2** ▲ Reserve 2 tablespoons of the sesame seeds. Spread the rest on a baking sheet and bake until lightly toasted, about 10 minutes.

**3** Sift the flour, salt and baking powder into a bowl.

**4** ▲ Stir in the toasted sesame seeds and set aside.

**5** With an electric mixer, cream the butter or margarine and sugar together until light and fluffy. Beat in the eggs, then stir in the lemon rind and milk.

**6** ▼ Pour the milk mixture over the dry ingredients and fold in with a large metal spoon until just blended.

**7** ▲ Pour into the tin and sprinkle over the reserved sesame seeds.

**8** Bake until a skewer inserted in the centre comes out clean, about 1 hour. Let cool in the tin for about 10 minutes. Turn out onto a wire rack to cool completely.

# Lemon and Walnut Tea Bread

**MAKES 1 LOAF**

4 oz (115 g) butter or margarine, at room
   temperature

3¹/₂ oz (100 g) sugar

2 eggs, at room temperature, separated

grated rind of 2 lemons

2 tablespoons lemon juice

7¹/₂ oz (215 g) plain flour

2 teaspoons baking powder

4 fl oz (125 ml) milk

2 oz (55 g) walnuts, chopped

¹/₈ teaspoon salt

**1**  Preheat a 350°F/180°C/Gas 4 oven.
Line a 9 × 5 in (23 × 13 cm) loaf tin
with greaseproof paper and grease.

**2**  With an electric mixer, cream the
butter or margarine with the sugar
until light and fluffy.

**3 ▲**  Beat in the egg yolks.

**4**  Add the lemon rind and juice and
stir until blended. Set aside.

**5 ▲**  In another bowl, sift together
the flour and baking powder, 3 times.
Fold into the butter mixture in 3
batches, alternating with the milk.
Fold in the walnuts. Set aside.

**6 ▲**  Beat the egg whites and salt
until stiff peaks form. Fold a large
dollop of the egg whites into the
walnut mixture to lighten it. Fold in
the remaining egg whites carefully
until just blended.

**7 ▲**  Pour the batter into the
prepared tin and bake until a skewer
inserted in the centre of the loaf
comes out clean, 45–50 minutes.
Let stand 5 minutes before turning
out onto a rack to cool completely.

# Yeast Breads

Though the pace of today's life may leave less time for baking, bread-making can be the best antidote. The process is simple yet infinitely variable, as the loaves that follow prove. Roll up your sleeves and create a tradition.

# White Bread

**MAKES 2 LOAVES**

| |
|---|
| 2 fl oz (65 ml) lukewarm water |
| 1 tablespoon active dried yeast |
| 2 tablespoons sugar |
| 16 fl oz (450 ml) lukewarm milk |
| 1 oz (30 g) butter or margarine, at room temperature |
| 2 teaspoons salt |
| 1 lb 14 oz–2 lbs (850–900 g) strong flour |

**1** Combine the water, dried yeast and 1 tablespoon of sugar in a measuring jug and leave to stand for 15 minutes until the mixture is frothy.

**2 ▼** Pour the milk into a large bowl. Add the remaining sugar, the butter or margarine, and salt. Stir in the yeast mixture.

**3** Stir in the flour, 5 oz (140 g) at a time, until a stiff dough is obtained. Alternatively, use a food processor.

**4 ▲** Transfer the dough to a floured surface. To knead, push the dough away from you with the palm of your hand, then fold it towards you, and push it away again. Repeat until the dough is smooth and elastic.

**5** Place the dough in a large greased bowl, cover with a plastic bag, and leave to rise in a warm place until doubled in volume, 2–3 hours.

**6** Grease 2 9 × 5 in (23 × 13 cm) tins.

**7 ▲** Punch down the risen dough with your fist and divide in half. Form into a loaf shape and place in the tins, seam-side down. Cover and let rise in a warm place until almost doubled in volume, about 45 minutes.

**8** Preheat a 375°F/190°C/Gas 5 oven.

**9** Bake until firm and brown, 45–50 minutes. Turn out and tap the bottom of a loaf: if it sounds hollow the loaf is done. If necessary, return to the oven and bake a few minutes more. Let cool on a rack.

# Multi-Grain Bread

**MAKES 2 LOAVES**

| |
|---|
| 1 tablespoon active dried yeast |
| 2 fl oz (65 ml) lukewarm water |
| 2¹/₂ oz (70 g) rolled oats (not quick cooking) |
| 16 fl oz (450 ml) milk |
| 2 teaspoons salt |
| 2 fl oz (65 ml) oil |
| 2 oz (55 g) light brown sugar |
| 2 tablespoons honey |
| 2 eggs, lightly beaten |
| 1 oz (30 g) wheat germ |
| 6 oz (170 g) soya flour |
| 12 oz (350 g) wholemeal flour |
| 15 oz–1 lb 1¹/₂ oz (420–490 g) strong flour |

**1**   Combine the yeast and water, stir, and leave for 15 minutes to dissolve.

**2 ▲**   Place the oats in a large bowl. Scald the milk, then pour over the rolled oats.

**3**   Stir in the salt, oil, sugar and honey. Leave until lukewarm.

~ VARIATION ~

Different flours may be used in this recipe, such as rye, barley, buckwheat or cornmeal. Try replacing the wheat germ and the soya flour with one or two of these, using the same total amount.

**4 ▲**   Stir in the yeast mixture, eggs, wheat germ, soya and wholemeal flours. Gradually stir in enough strong flour to obtain a rough dough.

**5**   Transfer the dough to a floured surface and knead, adding flour if necessary, until smooth and elastic. Return to a clean bowl, cover and leave to rise in a warm place until doubled in volume, about 2¹/₂ hours.

**6**   Grease 2 8¹/₂ × 4¹/₂ in (21.5 × 11.5 cm) bread tins. Punch down the risen dough and knead briefly.

**7**   Divide the dough into quarters. Roll each quarter into a cylinder 1¹/₂ in (3 cm) thick. Twist together 2 cylinders and place in a tin; repeat for remaining cylinders.

**8**   Cover and leave to rise until doubled in size, about 1 hour.

**9**   Preheat a 375°F/190°C/Gas 5 oven.

**10 ▲**   Bake for 45–50 minutes, until the bottoms sound hollow when tapped lightly. Cool on a rack.

# Plaited Loaf

## MAKES 1 LOAF

| |
|---|
| 1 tablespoon active dried yeast |
| 1 teaspoon honey |
| 8 fl oz (250 ml) lukewarm milk |
| 2 oz (55 g) butter, melted |
| 15 oz (420 g) strong flour |
| 1 teaspoon salt |
| 1 egg, lightly beaten |
| 1 egg yolk beaten with 1 teaspoon milk, for glazing |

**1 ▼** Combine the yeast, honey, milk and butter. Stir and leave for 15 minutes to dissolve.

**2** In a large bowl, mix together the flour and salt. Make a well in the centre and add the yeast mixture and egg. With a wooden spoon, stir from the centre, incorporating flour with each turn, to obtain a rough dough.

**3** Transfer to a floured surface and knead until smooth and elastic. Place in a clean bowl, cover and leave to rise in a warm place until doubled in volume, about 1½ hours.

**4** Grease a baking sheet. Punch down the dough and divide into three equal pieces. Roll to shape each piece into a long thin strip.

**5 ▲** Begin plaiting with the centre strip, tucking in the ends. Cover loosely and leave to rise in a warm place for 30 minutes.

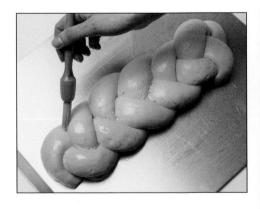

**6 ▲** Preheat a 375°F/190°C/Gas 5 oven. Place the bread in a cool place while the oven heats. Brush with the glaze and bake until golden, 40–45 minutes. Turn out onto a rack to cool.

# Oatmeal Bread

**MAKES 2 LOAVES**

| |
|---|
| 16 fl oz (450 ml) milk |
| 1 oz (30 g) butter |
| 2 oz (55 g) dark brown sugar |
| 2 teaspoons salt |
| 1 tablespoon active dried yeast |
| 2 fl oz (65 ml) lukewarm water |
| 13¾ oz (390 g) rolled oats (not quick-cooking) |
| 1 lb 8 oz–1 lb 14 oz (700–850 g) strong flour |

**1** ▲   Scald the milk. Remove from the heat and stir in the butter, brown sugar and salt. Leave until lukewarm.

**2**   Combine the yeast and warm water in a large bowl and leave until the yeast is dissolved and the mixture is frothy. Stir in the milk mixture.

**3** ▲   Add 10 oz (285 g) of the oats and enough flour to obtain a soft dough.

**4**   Transfer to a floured surface and knead until smooth and elastic.

**5** ▲   Place in a greased bowl, cover with a plastic bag, and leave until doubled in volume, 2–3 hours.

**6**   Grease a large baking sheet. Transfer the dough to a lightly floured surface and divide in half.

**7** ▼   Shape into rounds. Place on the baking sheet, cover with a tea towel and leave to rise until doubled in volume, about 1 hour.

**8**   Preheat a 400°F/200°C/Gas 6 oven. Score the tops and sprinkle with the remaining oats. Bake until the bottoms sound hollow when tapped, 45–50 minutes. Cool on racks.

# Pleated Rolls

**MAKES 48 ROLLS**

| |
|---|
| 1 tablespoon active dried yeast |
| 16 fl oz (450 ml) lukewarm milk |
| 4 oz (115 g) margarine |
| 5 tablespoons sugar |
| 2 teaspoons salt |
| 2 eggs |
| 2 lb 3 oz–2 lb 8 oz (985 g–1.2 kg) strong flour |
| 2 oz (55 g) butter |

**1** Combine the yeast and 4 fl oz (125 ml) milk in a large bowl. Stir and leave for 15 minutes to dissolve.

**2** Scald the remaining milk, cool for 5 minutes, then beat in the margarine, sugar, salt and eggs. Let cool to lukewarm.

**3 ▲** Pour the milk mixture into the yeast mixture. Stir in half the flour with a wooden spoon. Add the remaining flour, 5 oz (190 g) at a time, until a rough dough is obtained.

**4** Transfer the dough to a lightly floured surface and knead until smooth and elastic. Place in a clean bowl, cover with a plastic bag and leave to rise in a warm place until doubled in volume, about 2 hours.

**5** In a saucepan, melt the butter and set aside. Grease 2 baking sheets.

**6** Punch down the dough and divide into 4 equal pieces. Roll each piece into a 12 × 8 in (30 × 20 cm) rectangle, about ¼ in (5 mm) thick.

**7 ▲** Cut each of the rectangles into 4 long strips. Cut each strip into 3 4 × 2 in (10 × 5 cm) rectangles.

**8 ▲** Brush each rectangle with melted butter, then fold the rectangles in half, so that the top extends about ½ in (1 cm) over the bottom.

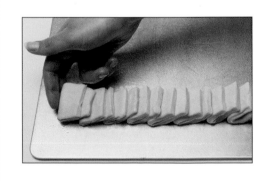

**9 ▲** Place the rectangles slightly overlapping on the baking sheet, with the longer side facing up.

**10** Cover and refrigerate for 30 minutes. Preheat a 350°F/180°C/Gas 4 oven. Bake until golden, 18–20 minutes. Cool slightly before serving.

# Cheese Bread

**MAKES 1 LOAF**

| |
|---|
| 1 tablespoon active dried yeast |
| 8 fl oz (250 ml) lukewarm milk |
| 1 oz (30 g) butter |
| 15 oz (420 g) strong flour |
| 2 teaspoons salt |
| 3½ oz (100 g) mature cheddar cheese, grated |

**1** Combine the yeast and milk. Stir and leave for 15 minutes to dissolve.

**2** Melt the butter, let cool, and add to the yeast mixture.

**3** Mix the flour and salt together in a large bowl. Make a well in the centre and pour in the yeast mixture.

**4** With a wooden spoon, stir from the centre, incorporating flour with each turn, to obtain a rough dough. If the dough seems too dry, add 2–3 tablespoons water.

**5** Transfer to a floured surface and knead until smooth and elastic. Return to the bowl, cover and leave to rise in a warm place until doubled in volume, 2–3 hours.

**6 ▲** Grease a 9 × 5 in (23 × 13 cm) bread tin. Punch down the dough with your fist. Knead in the cheese, distributing it as evenly as possible.

**7 ▼** Twist the dough, form into a loaf shape and place in the tin, tucking the ends under. Leave in a warm place until the dough rises above the rim of the tin.

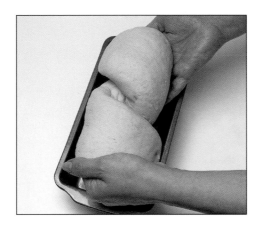

**8 ▲** Preheat a 400°F/200°C/Gas 6 oven. Bake for 15 minutes, then lower to 375°F/190°C/Gas 5 and bake until the bottom sounds hollow when tapped, about 30 minutes more.

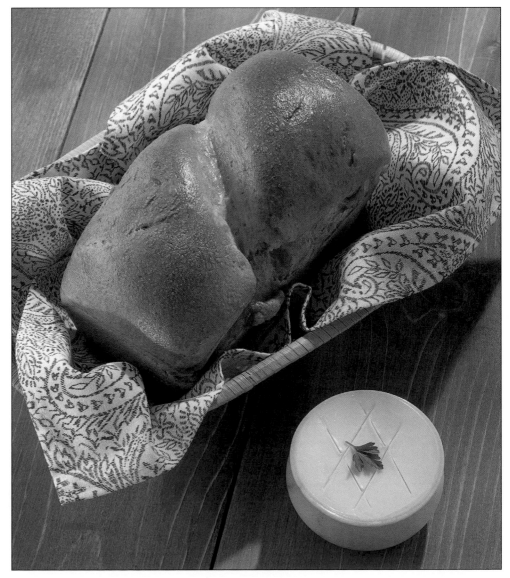

# Dill Bread

**MAKES 2 LOAVES**

| |
|---|
| 4 teaspoons active dried yeast |
| 16 fl oz (450 ml) lukewarm water |
| 2 tablespoons sugar |
| 2 lb 5½ oz (1.05 kg) strong flour |
| ½ onion, chopped |
| 4 tablespoons oil |
| 1 large bunch of dill, finely chopped |
| 2 eggs, lightly beaten |
| 5½ oz (150 g) cottage cheese |
| 4 teaspoons salt |
| milk, for glazing |

**1**   Mix together the yeast, water and sugar in a large bowl and leave for 15 minutes to dissolve.

**2** ▼   Stir in about half of the flour. Cover and leave to rise in a warm place for 45 minutes.

**3** ▲   In a frying pan, cook the onion in 1 tablespoon of the oil until soft. Set aside to cool, then stir into the yeast mixture. Stir the dill, eggs, cottage cheese, salt and remaining oil into the yeast. Gradually add the remaining flour until too stiff to stir.

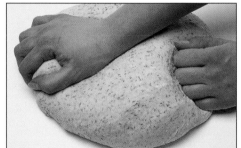

**4** ▲   Transfer to a floured surface and knead until smooth and elastic. Place in a bowl, cover and leave to rise until doubled in volume, 1–1½ hours.

**5** ▲   Grease a large baking sheet. Cut the dough in half and shape into 2 rounds. Leave to rise in a warm place for 30 minutes.

**6**   Preheat a 375°F/190°C/Gas 5 oven. Score the tops, brush with the milk and bake until browned, about 50 minutes. Cool on a rack.

# Spiral Herb Bread

**MAKES 2 LOAVES**

| |
|---|
| 2 tablespoons active dried yeast |
| 1 pt (600 ml) lukewarm water |
| 15 oz (420 g) strong flour |
| 1 lb 2 oz (505 g) wholemeal flour |
| 3 teaspoons salt |
| 1 oz (30 g) butter |
| 1 large bunch of parsley, finely chopped |
| 1 bunch of spring onions, chopped |
| 1 garlic clove, finely chopped |
| salt and freshly ground black pepper |
| 1 egg, lightly beaten |
| milk, for glazing |

**1**   Combine the yeast and 2 fl oz (65 ml) of the water, stir and leave for 15 minutes to dissolve.

**2**   Combine the flours and salt in a large bowl. Make a well in the centre and pour in the yeast mixture and the remaining water. With a wooden spoon, stir from the centre, working outwards to obtain a rough dough.

**3**   Transfer the dough to a floured surface and knead until smooth and elastic. Return to the bowl, cover with a plastic bag, and leave until doubled in volume, about 2 hours.

**4** ▲   Meanwhile, combine the butter, parsley, spring onions and garlic in a large frying pan. Cook over low heat, stirring, until softened. Season and set aside.

**5**   Grease 2 9 × 5 in (23 × 13 cm) tins. When the dough has risen, cut in half and roll each half into a rectangle about 14 × 9 in (35 × 23 cm).

**6** ▼   Brush both with the beaten egg. Divide the herb mixture between the two, spreading just up to the edges.

**7** ▲   Roll up to enclose the filling and pinch the short ends to seal. Place in the tins, seam-side down. Cover, and leave in a warm place until the dough rises above the rim of the tins.

**8**   Preheat a 375°F/190°C/Gas 5 oven. Brush with milk and bake until the bottoms sound hollow when tapped, about 55 minutes. Cool on a rack.

# Walnut Bread

**MAKES 1 LOAF**

| |
|---|
| 15 oz (420 g) wholemeal flour |
| 5 oz (140 g) strong flour |
| 2½ teaspoons salt |
| 18 fl oz (525 ml) lukewarm water |
| 1 tablespoon honey |
| 1 tablespoon active dried yeast |
| 5 oz (140 g) walnut pieces, plus more for decorating |
| 1 beaten egg, for glazing |

**1** Combine the flours and salt in a large bowl. Make a well in the centre and add 8 fl oz (250 ml) of the water, the honey and the yeast.

**2** Set aside until the yeast dissolves and the mixture is frothy.

**3** Add the remaining water. With a wooden spoon, stir from the centre, incorporating flour with each turn, to obtain a smooth dough. Add more flour if the dough is too sticky and use your hands if the dough becomes too stiff to stir.

**4** Transfer to a floured board and knead, adding flour if necessary, until the dough is smooth and elastic. Place in a greased bowl and roll the dough around in the bowl to coat thoroughly on all sides.

**5** ▲ Cover with a plastic bag and leave in a warm place until doubled in volume, about 1½ hours.

**6** ▲ Punch down the dough and knead in the walnuts evenly.

**7** Grease a baking sheet. Shape into a round loaf and place on the baking sheet. Press in walnut pieces to decorate the top. Cover loosely with a damp cloth and leave to rise in a warm place until doubled, 25–30 minutes.

**8** Preheat a 425°F/220°C/Gas 7 oven.

**9** ▲ With a sharp knife, score the top. Brush with the glaze. Bake for 15 minutes. Lower the heat to 375°F/190°C/Gas 5 and bake until the bottom sounds hollow when tapped, about 40 minutes. Cool on a rack.

# Pecan Rye Bread

**MAKES 2 LOAVES**

| |
|---|
| 1¹/₂ tablespoons active dried yeast |
| 24 fl oz (700 ml) lukewarm water |
| 1 lb 8 oz (700 g) strong flour |
| 1 lb 2 oz (500 g) rye flour |
| 2 tablespoons salt |
| 1 tablespoon honey |
| 2 teaspoons caraway seeds, (optional) |
| 4 oz (115 g) butter, at room temperature |
| 8 oz (225 g) pecans, chopped |

**1**   Combine the dried yeast and 4 fl oz (125 ml) of the lukewarm water. Stir and leave for 15 minutes to dissolve.

**2**   In the bowl of an electric mixer, combine the flours, salt, honey, caraway seeds and butter. With the dough hook, mix on low speed until well blended.

**3**   Add the yeast mixture and the remaining lukewarm water, then mix on medium speed until the dough forms a ball.

**4 ▲**   Transfer to a floured surface and knead in the pecans.

**5**   Return the dough to a bowl, cover with a plastic bag and leave in a warm place until doubled, about 2 hours.

**6**   Grease 2 8¹/₂ × 4¹/₂ in (21.5 × 11.5 cm) bread tins.

**7 ▲**   Punch down the risen dough.

**8**   Divide the dough in half and form into loaves. Place in the tins, seam side down. Dust the tops with flour.

**9**   Cover with plastic bags and leave to rise in a warm place until doubled in volume, about 1 hour.

**10**   Preheat a 375°F/190°C/Gas 5 oven.

**11 ▼**   Bake until the bottoms sound hollow when tapped, 45–50 minutes. Cool on racks.

# Sticky Buns

**MAKES 18**

| |
|---|
| 5¹/₂ fl oz (170 ml) milk |
| 1 tablespoon active dried yeast |
| 2 tablespoons caster sugar |
| 15 oz–1 lb (420–450 g) strong flour |
| 1 teaspoon salt |
| 4 oz (115 g) cold butter, cut into pieces |
| 2 eggs, lightly beaten |
| grated rind of 1 lemon |
| FOR THE TOPPING AND FILLING |
| 10 oz (285 g) dark brown sugar |
| 2¹/₂ oz (70 g) butter |
| 4 fl oz (125 ml) water |
| 3 oz (85 g) pecans or walnuts, chopped |
| 3 tablespoons caster sugar |
| 2 teaspoons ground cinnamon |
| 5¹/₂ oz (150 g) raisins |

**1** Heat the milk to lukewarm. Add the yeast and sugar and leave until frothy, about 15 minutes.

**2** Combine the flour and salt in a large mixing bowl. Add the butter and rub in with your fingertips until the mixture resembles coarse breadcrumbs.

**3 ▲** Make a well in the centre and add the yeast mixture, eggs and lemon rind. With a wooden spoon, stir from the centre, incorporating flour with each turn. When it becomes too stiff, stir by hand to obtain a rough dough.

**4** Transfer to a floured surface and knead until smooth and elastic. Return to the bowl, cover with a plastic bag and leave to rise in a warm place until doubled in volume, about 2 hours.

**5** Meanwhile, for the topping, make the syrup. Combine the brown sugar, butter and water in a heavy saucepan. Bring to the boil and boil gently until thick and syrupy, about 10 minutes.

**6 ▲** Place 1 tablespoon of the syrup in the bottom of each of 18 1¹/₂ in (4 cm) muffin cups. Sprinkle in a thin layer of chopped nuts, reserving the rest for the filling.

**7** Punch down the dough and transfer to a floured surface. Roll out to an 18 × 12 in (45 × 30 cm) rectangle.

**8 ▲** For the filling, combine the caster sugar, cinnamon, raisins and reserved nuts. Sprinkle over the dough in an even layer.

**9 ▲** Roll up tightly, from the long side, to form a cylinder.

**10 ▲** Cut the cylinder into 1 in (2.5 cm) rounds. Place each in a prepared muffin cup, cut-side up. Leave to rise in a warm place until increased by half, about 30 minutes.

**11** Preheat a 350°F/180°C/Gas 4 oven. Place foil under the tins to catch any syrup that bubbles over. Bake until golden, about 25 minutes.

**12** Remove from the oven and invert the tins onto a baking sheet. Leave for 3–5 minutes, then remove buns from the tins. Transfer to a rack to cool. Serve sticky-side up.

> **~ COOK'S TIP ~**
>
> To save time and energy, make double the recipe and freeze half for another occasion.

# Raisin Bread

**MAKES 2 LOAVES**

| |
|---|
| 1 tablespoon active dried yeast |
| 16 fl oz (450 ml) lukewarm milk |
| 5 oz (140 g) raisins |
| 2¹/₂ oz (70 g) currants |
| 1 tablespoon sherry or brandy |
| ¹/₂ teaspoon grated nutmeg |
| grated rind of 1 large orange |
| 2¹/₄ oz (60 g) sugar |
| 1 tablespoon salt |
| 4 oz (115 g) butter, melted |
| 1 lb 8 oz–1 lb 14 oz (700–850 g) strong flour |
| 1 egg beaten with 1 tablespoon cream, for glazing |

**1** Stir together the yeast and 4 fl oz (125 ml) of the milk and let stand for 15 minutes to dissolve.

**2** ▲ Mix the raisins, currants, sherry or brandy, nutmeg and orange rind together and set aside.

**3** In another bowl, mix the remaining milk, sugar, salt and half the butter. Add the yeast mixture. With a wooden spoon, stir in half the flour, 5 oz (140 g) at a time, until blended. Add the remaining flour as needed for a stiff dough.

**4** Transfer to a floured surface and knead until smooth and elastic. Place in a greased bowl, cover and leave to rise in a warm place until doubled in volume, about 2¹/₂ hours.

**5** Punch down the dough, return to the bowl, cover and leave to rise in a warm place for 30 minutes.

**6** Grease 2 8¹/₂ × 4¹/₂ in (21.5 × 11.5 cm) bread tins. Divide the dough in half and roll each half into a 20 × 7 in (50 × 18 cm) rectangle.

**7** ▲ Brush the rectangles with the remaining melted butter. Sprinkle over the raisin mixture, then roll up tightly, tucking in the ends slightly as you roll. Place in the prepared tins, cover, and leave to rise until almost doubled in volume.

**8** ▲ Preheat a 400°F/200°C/Gas 6 oven. Brush the loaves with the glaze. Bake for 20 minutes. Lower to 350°F/180°C/Gas 4 and bake until golden, 25–30 minutes more. Cool on racks.

# Prune Bread

**MAKES 1 LOAF**

| |
|---|
| 8 oz (225 g) dried prunes |
| 1 tablespoon active dried yeast |
| 3 oz (85 g) wholemeal flour |
| 13¹/₂–15 oz (385–420 g) strong flour |
| ¹/₂ teaspoon bicarbonate of soda |
| 1 teaspoon salt |
| 1 teaspoon pepper |
| 1 oz (30 g) butter, at room temperature |
| 6 fl oz (175 ml) buttermilk |
| 2 oz (55 g) walnuts, chopped |
| milk, for glazing |

**1**   Simmer the prunes in water to cover until soft, or soak overnight. Drain, reserving 2 fl oz (65 ml) of the soaking liquid. Stone and chop the prunes.

**2**   Combine the yeast and the reserved prune liquid, stir and leave for 15 minutes to dissolve.

**3**   In a large bowl, stir together the flours, bicarbonate of soda, salt and pepper. Make a well in the centre.

**4 ▲**   Add the chopped prunes, butter, and buttermilk. Pour in the yeast mixture. With a wooden spoon, stir from the centre, incorporating more flour with each turn, to obtain a rough dough.

**5**   Transfer to a floured surface and knead until smooth and elastic. Return to the bowl, cover with a plastic bag and leave to rise in a warm place until doubled in volume, about 1¹/₂ hours.

**6**   Grease a baking sheet.

**7 ▲**   Punch down the dough with your fist, then knead in the walnuts.

**8**   Shape the dough into a long, cylindrical loaf. Place on the baking sheet, cover loosely, and leave to rise in a warm place for 45 minutes.

**9**   Preheat a 425°F/220°C/Gas 7 oven.

**10 ▼**   With a sharp knife, score the top deeply. Brush with milk and bake for 15 minutes. Lower to 375°F/190°C/Gas 5 and bake until the bottom sounds hollow when tapped, about 35 minutes more. Cool.

# Danish Wreath

## SERVES 10–12

| |
| --- |
| ¹/₄ oz (7 g) active dried yeast |
| 6 fl oz (175 ml) lukewarm milk |
| 2 oz (55 g) caster sugar |
| 1 lb (450 g) strong flour |
| ¹/₂ teaspoon salt |
| ¹/₂ teaspoon vanilla essence |
| 1 egg, beaten |
| 2 × 4 oz (115 g) blocks unsalted butter |
| 1 egg yolk beaten with 2 teaspoons water, for glazing |
| 4 oz (115 g) icing sugar |
| 1–2 tablespoons water |
| chopped pecans or walnuts, for sprinkling |
| FOR THE FILLING |
| 7 oz (200 g) dark brown sugar |
| 1 teaspoon ground cinnamon |
| 2 oz (55 g) pecans or walnuts, toasted and chopped |

**1** Combine the yeast, milk and ¹/₂ teaspoon of the sugar. Stir and leave for 15 minutes to dissolve.

**2** Combine the flour, sugar and salt. Make a well in the centre and add the yeast mixture, vanilla and egg. Stir until a rough dough is formed.

**3** Transfer to a floured surface and knead until smooth and elastic. Wrap and refrigerate for 15 minutes.

---

### ~ VARIATION ~

For a different filling, substitute 3 tart apples, peeled and grated, the grated rind of 1 lemon, 1 tablespoon lemon juice, ¹/₂ teaspoon ground cinnamon, 3 tablespoons sugar, 1¹/₄ oz (35 g) currants, and 1 oz (30 g) chopped walnuts. Combine well and use as described.

---

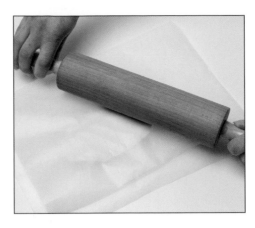

**4** ▲ Meanwhile, place the butter between two sheets of greaseproof paper. With a rolling pin, flatten to form 2 6 × 4 in (15 × 10 cm) rectangles. Set aside.

**5** ▲ Roll out the dough to a 12 × 8 in (30 × 20 cm) rectangle. Place one butter rectangle in the centre. Fold the bottom third of dough over the butter and seal the edge. Place the other butter rectangle on top and cover with the top third of the dough.

**6** Turn the dough so the shorter side faces you. Roll into a 12 × 8 in (30 × 20 cm) rectangle. Fold into thirds, and indent one edge with your finger to indicate the first turn. Wrap in clear film and refrigerate for 30 minutes.

**7** Repeat two more times; rolling, folding, marking and chilling between each turn. After the third fold refrigerate for 1–2 hours, or longer.

**8** Grease a large baking sheet. In a bowl, stir together all the filling ingredients until blended.

**9** ▲ Roll out the dough to a 25 × 6 in (3 × 15 cm) strip. Spread over the filling, leaving a ¹/₂ in (1 cm) border.

**10** Roll up the dough lengthways into a cylinder. Place on the baking sheet and form into a circle, pinching the edges together to seal. Cover with an inverted bowl and leave in a warm place to rise for 45 minutes.

**11** ▲ Preheat the oven to 400°F/ 200°C/Gas 6. Slash the top every 2 in (5 cm), cutting about ¹/₂ in (1 cm) deep. Brush with the egg glaze. Bake until golden, 35–40 minutes. Cool on a rack. To serve, mix the icing sugar and water, then drizzle over the wreath. Sprinkle with the pecans or walnuts.

# Kugelhopf

**MAKES 1 LOAF**

3³/₄ oz (110 g) raisins

1 tablespoon kirsch or brandy

1 tablespoon active dried yeast

4 fl oz (125 ml) lukewarm water

4 oz (115 g) unsalted butter, at room temperature

3¹/₂ oz (100 g) sugar

3 eggs, at room temperature

grated rind of 1 lemon

1 teaspoon salt

¹/₂ teaspoon vanilla essence

15 oz (420 g) strong flour

4 fl oz (125 ml) milk

1 oz (30 g) flaked almonds

3¹/₄ oz (90 g) whole blanched almonds, chopped

icing sugar, for dusting

**1 ▼** In a bowl, combine the raisins and kirsch or brandy. Set aside.

**2** Combine the yeast and water, stir and leave for 15 minutes to dissolve.

**3** With an electric mixer, cream the butter and sugar until thick and fluffy. Beat in the eggs, one at a time. Add the lemon rind, salt and vanilla. Stir in the yeast mixture.

**4 ▲** Add the flour, alternating with the milk, until the mixture is well blended. Cover and leave to rise in a warm place until doubled in volume, about 2 hours.

**5 ▲** Grease a 4¹/₂ pt kugelhopf mould, then sprinkle the flaked almonds evenly over the bottom.

**6** Work the raisins and almonds into the dough, then spoon into the mould. Cover with a plastic bag, and leave to rise in a warm place until the dough almost reaches the top of the tin, about 1 hour.

**7** Preheat a 350°F/180°C/Gas 4 oven.

**8** Bake until golden brown, for about 45 minutes. If the top browns too quickly, protect it with a sheet of foil. Allow to cool in the tin for 15 minutes, then turn out onto a rack. Dust the top lightly with icing sugar before serving.

# Pies & Tarts

Here you will find every sort of filling for the most memorable
pies and tarts – from orchard fruits to autumn nuts, and from
tangy citrus to luscious chocolate. Some are plain and
some are fancy, but all are delicious.

# Peach Leaf Pie

**SERVES 8**

| |
|---|
| 2 lb 8 oz (1.2 kg) ripe peaches |
| juice of 1 lemon |
| 3½ oz (100 g) sugar |
| 3 tablespoons cornflour |
| ¼ teaspoon grated nutmeg |
| ½ teaspoon ground cinnamon |
| 1 oz (30 g) butter, diced |

**FOR THE CRUST**

| |
|---|
| 10 oz (285 g) plain flour |
| ¾ teaspoon salt |
| 4 oz (115 g) cold butter, cut into pieces |
| 2¼ oz (60 g) cold vegetable fat or lard, cut into pieces |
| 5–6 tablespoons iced water |
| 1 egg beaten with 1 tablespoon water, for glazing |

**1** For the pastry, sift the flour and salt into a bowl. Add the butter and fat and rub in with your fingertips until the mixture resembles coarse breadcrumbs.

**2 ▲** With a fork, stir in just enough water to bind the dough. Gather into 2 balls, one slightly larger than the other. Wrap in clear film and refrigerate for at least 20 minutes.

**3** Place a baking sheet in the oven and preheat to 425°F/220°C/Gas 7.

**4 ▲** Drop a few peaches at a time into boiling water for 20 seconds, then transfer to a bowl of cold water. When cool, peel off the skins.

**5** Slice the peaches and combine with the lemon juice, sugar, cornstarch and spices. Set aside.

**6 ▲** On a lightly floured surface, roll out the larger dough ball about ⅛ in (3 mm) thick. Transfer to a 9 in (23 cm) pie tin and trim. Refrigerate.

**7 ▲** Roll out the remaining dough ¼ in (5 mm) thick. Cut out leaf shapes 3 in (8 cm) long, using a template if needed. Mark veins with a knife. With the scraps, roll a few balls.

**8 ▲** Brush the bottom of the pastry shell with egg glaze. Add the peaches, piling them higher in the centre. Dot with the butter.

**9 ▲** To assemble, start from the outside edge and cover the peaches with a ring of leaves. Place a second ring of leaves above, staggering the positions. Continue with rows of leaves until covered. Place the balls in the centre. Brush with glaze.

**10** Bake for 10 minutes. Lower the heat to 350°F/180°C/Gas 4 and bake for 35–40 minutes more.

### ~ COOK'S TIP ~

Baking the pie on a preheated baking sheet helps to make the bottom crust crisp. The moisture from the filling keeps the bottom crust more humid than the top, but this baking method helps to compensate for the top crust being better exposed to the heat source.

# Apple and Cranberry Lattice Pie

**SERVES 8**

| |
|---|
| grated rind of 1 orange |
| 3 tablespoons fresh orange juice |
| 2 large, tart cooking apples |
| 6 oz (170 g) cranberries |
| 2½ oz (70 g) raisins |
| 1 oz (30 g) walnuts, chopped |
| 7½ oz (215 g) caster sugar |
| 4 oz (115 g) dark brown sugar |
| 2 tablespoons plain flour |
| FOR THE CRUST |
| 10 oz (285 g) plain flour |
| ½ teaspoon salt |
| 3 oz (85 g) cold butter, cut into pieces |
| 3 oz (85 g) cold vegetable fat or lard, cut into pieces |
| 2–4 fl oz (65–125 ml) iced water |

1 ▼ For the crust, sift the flour and salt into a bowl. Add the butter and fat and rub in with your fingertips until the mixture resembles coarse breadcrumbs. With a fork, stir in just enough water to bind the dough. Gather into 2 equal balls, wrap in cling film, and refrigerate for at least 20 minutes.

2 ▲ Put the orange rind and juice into a mixing bowl. Peel and core the apples and grate into the bowl. Stir in the cranberries, raisins, walnuts, all except 1 tablespoon of the caster sugar, the brown sugar and flour.

3 Place a baking sheet in the oven and preheat to 400°F/200°C/Gas 6.

4 On a lightly floured surface, roll out 1 ball of dough about ⅛ in (3mm) thick. Transfer to a 9 in (23 cm) pie plate and trim. Spoon the cranberry and apple mixture into the shell.

5 ▲ Roll out the remaining dough to a circle about 11 in (28 cm) in diameter. With a serrated pastry wheel, cut the dough into 10 strips, ¾ in (2 cm) wide. Place 5 strips horizontally across the top of the tart at 1 in (2.5 cm) intervals. Weave in 5 vertical strips and trim. Sprinkle the top with the remaining sugar.

6 Bake the pie for 20 minutes. Reduce the heat to 350°F/180°C/ Gas 4 and bake for about 15 minutes more, until the crust is golden and the filling is bubbling.

# Open Apple Pie

**SERVES 8**

| |
|---|
| 3 lb (1.4 kg) sweet-tart firm eating or cooking apples |
| 1³/₄ oz (50 g) sugar |
| 2 teaspoons ground cinnamon |
| grated rind and juice of 1 lemon |
| 1 oz (30 g) butter, diced |
| 2–3 tablespoons honey |
| FOR THE CRUST |
| 10 oz (285 g) plain flour |
| ¹/₂ teaspoon salt |
| 4 oz (115 g) cold butter, cut into pieces |
| 2¹/₄ oz (60 g) cold vegetable fat or lard, cut into pieces |
| 5–6 tablespoons iced water |

**1** For the crust, sift the flour and salt into a bowl. Add the butter and fat and rub in with your fingertips until the mixture resembles coarse breadcrumbs.

**2** ▲ With a fork, stir in just enough water to bind the dough. Gather into a ball, wrap in clear film, and refrigerate for at least 20 minutes.

**3** Place a baking sheet in the centre of the oven and preheat to 400°F/200°C/Gas 6.

**4** ▼ Peel, core, and slice the apples. Combine the sugar and cinnamon in a bowl. Add the apples, lemon rind and juice and stir.

**5** On a lightly floured surface, roll out the dough to a circle about 12 in (30 cm) in diameter. Transfer to a 9 in (23 cm) diameter deep pie dish; leave the dough hanging over the edge. Fill with the apple slices.

**6** ▲ Fold in the edges and crimp loosely for a decorative border. Dot the apples with diced butter.

**7** Bake on the hot sheet until the pastry is golden and the apples are tender, about 45 minutes.

**8** Melt the honey in a saucepan and brush over the apples to glaze. Serve warm or at room temperature.

# Chocolate Lemon Tart

**SERVES 8–10**

| |
|---|
| 8³/₄ oz (240 g) caster sugar |
| 6 eggs |
| grated rind of 2 lemons |
| 5¹/₂ fl oz (170 ml) fresh lemon juice |
| 5¹/₂ fl oz (170 ml) whipping cream |
| chocolate curls, for decorating |
| FOR THE CRUST |
| 6¹/₄ oz (180 g) plain flour |
| 2 tablespoons unsweetened cocoa powder |
| 1 oz (30 g) icing sugar |
| ¹/₂ teaspoon salt |
| 4 oz (115 g) butter or margarine |
| 1 tablespoon water |

**1** ▲ Grease a 10 in (25 cm) tart tin.

**2** For the crust, sift the flour, cocoa powder, icing sugar and salt into a bowl. Set aside.

**3** ▲ Melt the butter and water over a low heat. Pour over the flour mixture and stir with a wooden spoon until the dough is smooth and the flour has absorbed all the liquid.

**4** Press the dough evenly over the base and side of the prepared tart tin. Refrigerate the tart shell while preparing the filling.

**5** Preheat a baking sheet in a 375°F/190°C/Gas 5 oven.

**6** ▲ Whisk the sugar and eggs until the sugar is dissolved. Add the lemon rind and juice and mix well. Add the cream. Taste the mixture and add more lemon juice or sugar if needed. It should taste tart but also sweet.

**7** Pour the filling into the tart shell and bake on the hot sheet until the filling is set, 20–25 minutes. Cool on a rack. When cool, decorate with the chocolate curls.

# Lemon Almond Tart

**SERVES 8**

5¹/₂ oz (150 g) whole blanched almonds

3¹/₂ oz (100 g) sugar

2 eggs

grated rind and juice of 1¹/₂ lemons

4 oz (115 g) butter, melted

strips of lemon rind, for decorating

FOR THE CRUST

6¹/₄ oz (180 g) plain flour

1 tablespoon sugar

¹/₂ teaspoon salt

¹/₂ teaspoon baking powder

3 oz (85 g) cold unsalted butter, cut into pieces

3–4 tablespoons whipping cream

**1** For the crust, sift the flour, sugar, salt and baking powder into a bowl. Add the butter and rub in with your fingertips until the mixture resembles coarse breadcrumbs.

**2 ▲** With a fork, stir in just enough cream to bind the dough.

**3** Gather into a ball and transfer to a lightly floured surface. Roll out the dough about ¹/₈ in (3 mm) thick and carefully transfer to a 9 in (23 cm) tart tin. Trim and prick the base all over with a fork. Refrigerate for at least 20 minutes.

**4** Preheat a baking sheet in a 400°F/ 200°C/Gas 6 oven.

**5** Line the tart shell with crumpled greaseproof paper and fill with dried beans. Bake for 12 minutes. Remove the paper and beans and continue baking until golden, 6–8 minutes more. Reduce the oven temperature to 350°F/180°C/Gas 4.

**6 ▲** Grind the almonds finely with 1 tablespoon of the sugar in a food processor, blender, or coffee grinder.

**7 ▲** Set a mixing bowl over a pan of hot water. Add the eggs and the remaining sugar, and beat with an electric mixer until the mixture is thick enough to leave a ribbon trail when the beaters are lifted.

**8** Stir in the lemon rind and juice, butter and ground almonds.

**9** Pour into the prebaked shell. Bake until the filling is golden and set, about 35 minutes. Decorate with lemon rind.

# Orange Tart

SERVES 8

| | |
|---|---|
| 7 oz (200 g) sugar | |
| 8 fl oz (250 ml) fresh orange juice, strained | |
| 2 large navel oranges | |
| 5½ oz (150 g) whole blanched almonds | |
| 2 oz (55 g) butter | |
| 1 egg | |
| 1 tablespoon plain flour | |
| 3 tablespoons apricot jam | |

FOR THE CRUST

| | |
|---|---|
| 7½ oz (215 g) plain flour | |
| ½ teaspoon salt | |
| 2 oz (55 g) cold butter, cut into pieces | |
| 1½ oz (45 g) cold margarine, cut into pieces | |
| 3–4 tablespoons iced water | |

**1** For the crust, sift the flour and salt into a bowl. Add the butter and margarine and rub in with your fingertips until the mixture resembles coarse breadcrumbs. Stir in just enough water to bind the dough. Gather into a ball, wrap in clear film, and refrigerate for at least 20 minutes.

**2** On a lightly floured surface, roll out the dough ¼ in (5 mm) thick and transfer to an 8 in (20 cm) tart tin. Trim off the overhang. Refrigerate until needed.

**3** In a saucepan, combine 5½ oz (150 g) of the sugar and the orange juice and boil until thick and syrupy, about 10 minutes.

**4** ▲ Cut the oranges into ¼ in (5 mm) slices. Do not peel. Add to the syrup. Simmer gently for 10 minutes, or until glazed. Transfer to a rack to dry. When cool, cut in half. Reserve the syrup. Place a baking sheet in the oven and heat to 400°F/200°C/Gas 6.

**5** Grind the almonds finely in a food processor, blender or coffee grinder. With an electric mixer, cream the butter and remaining sugar until light and fluffy. Beat in the egg and 2 tablespoons of the orange syrup. Stir in the almonds and flour.

**6** Melt the jam over low heat, then brush over the tart shell. Pour in the almond mixture. Bake until set, about 20 minutes. Let cool.

**7** ▲ Arrange overlapping orange slices on top. Boil the remaining syrup until thick. Brush on top to glaze.

# Cherry Strudel

**SERVES 8**

| |
| --- |
| 2¹/₂ oz (70 g) fresh breadcrumbs |
| 6 oz (170 g) butter, melted |
| 7 oz (200 g) sugar |
| 1 tablespoon ground cinnamon |
| 1 teaspoon grated lemon rind |
| 1 lb (450 g) sour cherries, stoned |
| 8 sheets filo pastry |
| icing sugar, for dusting |

**1** In a frying pan, lightly fry the fresh breadcrumbs in 2¹/₂ oz (70 g) of the melted butter until golden. Set aside to cool.

**2 ▲** In a large mixing bowl, toss together the sugar, cinnamon and lemon rind.

**3** Stir in the cherries.

**4** Preheat the oven to 375°F/190°C/ Gas 5. Grease a baking sheet.

**5** Carefully unfold the filo sheets. Keep the unused sheets covered with damp kitchen paper. Lift off one sheet, place on a flat surface lined with parchment paper. Brush the pastry with melted butter. Sprinkle about an eighth of the breadcrumbs evenly over the surface.

**6 ▲** Lay a second sheet of filo on top, brush with butter and sprinkle with crumbs. Continue until you have a stack of 8 buttered, crumbed sheets.

**7** Spoon the cherry mixture at the bottom edge of the strip. Starting at the cherry-filled end, roll up the dough as for a Swiss roll. Use the paper to help flip the strudel onto the baking sheet, seam-side down.

**8 ▼** Carefully fold under the ends to seal in the fruit. Brush the top with any remaining butter.

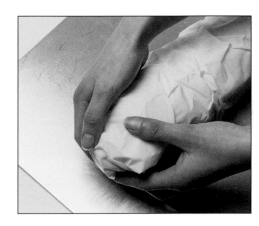

**9** Bake the strudel for 45 minutes. Let cool slightly. Using a small sieve, dust with a fine layer of icing sugar.

# Black Bottom Pie

**SERVES 8**

| |
|---|
| 2 teaspoons gelatin |
| 3 tablespoons cold water |
| 2 eggs, separated |
| 5 oz (140 g) caster sugar |
| 1/2 oz (15 g) cornflour |
| 1/2 teaspoon salt |
| 16 fl oz (450 ml) milk |
| 2 oz (55 g) plain chocolate, finely chopped |
| 2 tablespoons rum |
| 1/4 teaspoon cream of tartar |
| chocolate curls, for decorating |
| FOR THE CRUST |
| 6 oz (170 g) gingersnaps, crushed |
| 2 1/2 oz (70 g) butter, melted |

**1** Preheat a 350°F/180°C/Gas 4 oven.

**2** For the crust, mix the crushed gingersnaps and melted butter.

**3** ▲ Press the mixture evenly over the bottom and side of a 9 in (23 cm) pie plate. Bake for 6 minutes.

**4** Sprinkle the gelatin over the water and let stand to soften.

**5** Beat the egg yolks in a large mixing bowl and set aside.

**6** In a saucepan, combine half the sugar, the cornflour and salt. Gradually stir in the milk. Boil for 1 minute, stirring constantly.

**7** ▲ Whisk the hot milk mixture into the yolks, then pour all back into the saucepan and return to the boil, whisking. Cook for 1 minute, still whisking. Remove from the heat.

**8** ▲ Measure out 8 oz (225 g) of the hot custard mixture and pour into a bowl. Add the chopped chocolate to the custard mixture, and stir until melted. Stir in half the rum and pour into the pie shell.

**9** ▲ Whisk the softened gelatin into the plain custard until it has dissolved, then stir in the remaining rum. Set the pan in cold water until it reaches room temperature.

**10** ▲ With an electric mixer, beat the egg whites and cream of tartar until they hold stiff peaks. Add the remaining sugar gradually, beating or whisking thoroughly at each addition.

**11** ▲ Fold the custard into the egg whites, then spoon over the chocolate mixture in the pie shell. Refrigerate until set, about 2 hours.

**12** Decorate the top with chocolate curls. Keep the pie refrigerated until ready to serve.

### ~ COOK'S TIP ~

To make chocolate curls, melt 8 oz (225 g) plain chocolate over hot water, stir in 1 tablespoon of vegetable fat and mould in a small foil-lined loaf tin. For large curls, soften the bar between your hands and scrape off curls from the wide side with a vegetable peeler; for small curls, grate from the narrow side using a box grater.

# Glacé Fruit Pie

**SERVES 10**

| |
|---|
| 1 tablespoon rum |
| 2 oz (55 g) mixed glacé fruit, chopped |
| 16 fl oz (450 ml) milk |
| 4 teaspoons gelatin |
| 3½ oz (100 g) sugar |
| ½ teaspoon salt |
| 3 eggs, separated |
| 8 fl oz (250 ml) whipping cream |
| chocolate curls, for decorating |
| FOR THE CRUST |
| 6 oz (170 g) digestive biscuits, crushed |
| 2½ oz (70 g) butter, melted |
| 1 tablespoon sugar |

**1** For the crust, mix the crushed digestive biscuits, butter and sugar. Press evenly and firmly over the bottom and side of a 9 in (23 cm) pie plate. Refrigerate until firm.

**2** ▲ In a bowl, stir together the rum and glacé fruit. Set aside.

**3** Pour 4 fl oz (125 ml) of the milk into a small bowl. Sprinkle over the gelatin and let stand 5 minutes to soften.

**4** ▲ In the top of a double boiler, combine 1¾ oz (50 g) of the sugar, the remaining milk and salt. Stir in the gelatin mixture. Cook over hot water, stirring, until gelatin dissolves.

**5** Whisk in the egg yolks and cook, stirring, until thick enough to coat a spoon. Do not boil. Pour the custard over the glacé fruit mixture. Set in a bowl of ice water to cool.

**6** Whip the cream lightly. Set aside.

**7** With an electric mixer, beat the egg whites until they hold soft peaks. Add the remaining sugar and beat just enough to blend. Fold in a large dollop of the egg whites into the cooled gelatin mixture. Pour into the remaining egg whites and carefully fold together. Fold in the cream.

**8** ▲ Pour into the pie shell and chill until firm. Decorate the top with chocolate curls.

# Chocolate Chiffon Pie

**SERVES 8**

| |
|---|
| 7 oz (200 g) plain chocolate |
| 8 fl oz (250 ml) milk |
| 1 tablespoon gelatin |
| 3¹/₂ oz (100 g) sugar |
| 2 extra-large eggs, separated |
| 1 teaspoon vanilla essence |
| 12 fl oz (350 ml) whipping cream |
| ¹/₈ teaspoon salt |
| whipped cream and chocolate curls, for decorating |
| FOR THE CRUST |
| 7 oz (200 g) digestive biscuits, crushed |
| 3 oz (85 g) butter, melted |

1 Place a baking sheet in the oven and preheat to 350°F/180°C/ Gas 4.

2 For the crust, mix the crushed digestive biscuits and butter in a bowl. Press evenly over the bottom and side of a 9 in (23 cm) pie plate. Bake for 8 minutes. Let cool.

3 Chop the chocolate, then grate in a food processor or blender. Set aside.

4 Place the milk in the top of a double boiler. Sprinkle over the gelatin. Let stand 5 minutes to soften.

5 ▲ Set the top of a double boiler over hot water. Add 1¹/₂ oz (45 g) sugar, the chocolate and the egg yolks. Stir until dissolved. Add the vanilla essence.

6 ▲ Set the top of the double boiler in a bowl of ice and stir until the mixture reaches room temperature. Remove from the ice and set aside.

7 Whip the cream lightly. Set aside. With an electric mixer, beat the egg whites and salt until they hold soft peaks. Add the remaining sugar and beat only enough to blend.

8 Fold a dollop of egg whites into the chocolate mixture, then pour back into the whites and fold in.

9 ▲ Fold in the whipped cream and pour into the pie shell. Put in the freezer until just set, about 5 minutes. If the centre sinks, fill with any remaining mixture. Refrigerate for 3–4 hours. Decorate with whipped cream and chocolate curls. Serve cold.

# Mushroom Quiche

**SERVES 8**

| |
|---|
| 1 lb (450 g) mushrooms |
| 2 tablespoons olive oil |
| 1 tablespoon butter |
| 1 clove garlic, finely chopped |
| 1 tablespoon lemon juice |
| salt and pepper |
| 2 tablespoons finely chopped parsley |
| 3 eggs |
| 12 fl oz (300 ml) whipping cream |
| 2¼ oz (60 g) Parmesan cheese, grated |
| FOR THE CRUST |
| 6¼ (180 g) plain flour |
| ½ teaspoon salt |
| 3 oz (85 g) cold butter, cut into pieces |
| 1½ oz (45 g) cold margarine, cut into pieces |
| 3–4 tablespoons iced water |

**1** For the crust, sift the flour and salt into a bowl. Rub in the butter and margarine until the mixture resembles coarse breadcrumbs. Stir in just enough water to bind.

**2** Gather into a ball, wrap in clear film and refrigerate for 20 minutes.

**3** Preheat a baking sheet in a 375°F/190°C/Gas 5 oven.

**4** Roll out the dough ⅛ in (3 mm) thick. Transfer to a 9 in (23 cm) tart tin and trim. Prick the base all over with a fork. Line with greaseproof paper and fill with dried beans. Bake for 12 minutes. Remove the paper and beans and continue baking until golden, about 5 minutes more.

**5** ▲ Wipe the mushrooms with damp kitchen paper to remove any dirt. Trim the ends of the stalks, place on a cutting board, and slice thinly.

**6** Heat the oil and butter in a frying pan. Stir in the mushrooms, garlic and lemon juice. Season with salt and pepper. Cook until the mushrooms render their liquid, then raise the heat and cook until dry.

**7** ▼ Stir in the parsley and add more salt and pepper if necessary.

**8** Whisk the eggs and cream together, then stir in the mushrooms. Sprinkle the cheese over the bottom of the prebaked shell and pour the mushroom filling over the top.

**9** Bake until puffed and brown, about 30 minutes. Serve the quiche warm.

# Bacon and Cheese Quiche

**SERVES 8**

| |
|---|
| 4 oz (115 g) medium-thick bacon slices |
| 3 eggs |
| 12 fl oz (350 ml) whipping cream |
| 3½ oz (100 g) Gruyère cheese, grated |
| ⅛ teaspoon grated nutmeg |
| salt and pepper |
| FOR THE CRUST |
| 6¼ oz (180 g) plain flour |
| ½ teaspoon salt |
| 3 oz (85 g) cold butter, cut into pieces |
| 1½ oz (45 g) cold margarine, cut into pieces |
| 3–4 tablespoons iced water |

**1** Make the crust as directed in steps 1–4 above. Maintain the oven temperature at 375°F/190°C/Gas 5.

**2** ▲ Fry the bacon until crisp. Drain, then crumble into small pieces. Sprinkle in the pastry shell.

**3** ▲ Beat together the eggs, cream, cheese, nutmeg, salt and pepper. Pour over the bacon and bake until puffed and brown, about 30 minutes. Serve the quiche warm.

*Mushroom Quiche (top), Bacon and Cheese Quiche*

# Cheesy Tomato Quiche

**SERVES 6–8**

10 medium tomatoes

1 × 2 oz (55 g) can anchovy fillets, drained and finely chopped

4 fl oz (125 ml) whipping cream

7 oz (200 g) mature Cheddar cheese, grated

1 oz (30 g) wholemeal breadcrumbs

$^1\!/_2$ teaspoon dried thyme

salt and pepper

FOR THE CRUST

$7^1\!/_2$ oz (215 g) plain flour

4 oz (115 g) cold butter, cut into pieces

1 egg yolk

2–3 tablespoons iced water

**1** Preheat the oven to 400°F/200°C/ Gas 6.

**2** For the crust, sift the flour into a bowl. Rub in the butter with your fingertips until the mixture resembles coarse breadcrumbs.

**3** ▲ With a fork, stir in the egg yolk and enough water to bind the dough.

**4** Roll out the dough about $^1\!/_8$ in (3 mm) thick and transfer to a 9 in (23 cm) tart tin. Refrigerate until needed.

**5** ▲ Score the bottoms of the tomatoes. Plunge in boiling water for 1 minute. Remove and peel off the skin with a knife. Cut in quarters and remove the seeds with a spoon.

**6** ▲ In a bowl, mix the anchovies and cream. Stir in the cheese.

**7** Sprinkle the breadcrumbs in the tart. Arrange the tomatoes on top. Season with thyme, salt and pepper.

**8** ▲ Spoon the cheese mixture on top. Bake until golden, 25–30 minutes. Serve warm.

# Onion and Anchovy Tart

SERVES 8

| 4 tablespoons olive oil |
| 2 lb (900 g) onions, sliced |
| 1 teaspoon dried thyme |
| salt and pepper |
| 2–3 tomatoes, sliced |
| 24 small black olives, stoned |
| 1 × 2 oz (55 g) can anchovy fillets, drained and sliced |
| 6 sun-dried tomatoes, cut into slivers |
| FOR THE CRUST |
| 6¼ oz (180 g) plain flour |
| ½ teaspoon salt |
| 4 oz (115 g) cold butter, cut into pieces |
| 1 egg yolk |
| 2–3 tablespoons iced water |

**3** ▲ Heat the oil in a frying pan. Add the onions, thyme and seasoning. Cook over low heat, covered, for 25 minutes. Uncover and continue cooking until soft. Let cool. Preheat the oven to 400°F/200°C/Gas 6.

**4** ▼ Spoon the onions into the tart shell and top with the tomato slices. Arrange the olives in rows. Make a lattice pattern, alternating lines of anchovies and sun-dried tomatoes. Bake until golden, 20–25 minutes.

**1** ▲ For the crust, sift the flour and salt into a bowl. Rub in the butter with your fingertips until the mixture resembles coarse breadcrumbs. Stir in the yolk and enough water to bind.

**2** ▲ Roll out the dough to a thickness of about ⅛ in (3 mm). Transfer to a 9 in (23 cm) tart tin and trim the edge. Chill in the refrigerator until needed.

# Ricotta and Basil Tart

**SERVES 8–10**

2 oz (55 g) basil leaves

1 oz (30 g) flat-leaf parsley

4 fl oz (125 ml) extra-virgin olive oil

salt and pepper

2 eggs

1 egg yolk

1 lb 12 oz (800 g) ricotta cheese

3½ oz (100 g) black olives, stoned

2¼ oz (60 g) Parmesan cheese, freshly grated

FOR THE CRUST

6½ oz (180 g) plain flour

½ teaspoon salt

3 oz (85 g) cold butter, cut into pieces

1½ oz (45 g) cold margarine, cut into pieces

3–4 tablespoon iced water

**1** ▲ For the crust, combine the flour and salt in a bowl. Add the butter and margarine.

**2** Rub in with your fingertips until the mixture resembles coarse breadcrumbs. With a fork, stir in just enough water to bind the dough. Gather into a ball, wrap in clear film, and refrigerate for at least 20 minutes.

**3** Preheat a baking sheet in a 375°F/190°C/Gas 5 oven.

**4** Roll out the dough ⅛ in (3 mm) thick and transfer to a 10 in (25 cm) tart tin. Prick the base with a fork and line with greaseproof paper. Fill with dried beans and bake for 12 minutes. Remove the paper and beans and bake until golden, 3–5 minutes more. Lower the heat to 350°F/180°C/Gas 4.

**5** ▲ In a food processor, combine the basil, parsley and olive oil. Season well with salt and pepper and process until finely chopped.

**6** In a bowl, whisk the eggs and yolk to blend. Gently fold in the ricotta.

**7** ▲ Fold in the basil mixture and olives until well combined. Stir in the Parmesan and adjust the seasoning.

**8** Pour into the prebaked shell and bake until set, 30–35 minutes.

# Cakes & Gâteaux

As tasty as they are beautiful, these cakes and gâteaux will make any occasion memorable, whether you are looking for the homespun charm of a cheesecake or the sophisticated style of Sachertorte.

# Angel Cake

**SERVES 12–14**

4½ oz (125 g) sifted plain flour

2 tablespoons cornflour

10½ oz (300 g) caster sugar

10–11 oz (285–310 g) egg whites (about 10–11 eggs)

1¼ teaspoons cream of tartar

¼ teaspoon salt

1 teaspoon vanilla essence

¼ teaspoon almond essence

icing sugar, for dusting

**1** Preheat the oven to 325°F/170°C/ Gas 3.

**2** ▼ Sift the flours before measuring, then sift them 4 times with 3½ oz (100 g) of the sugar.

**3** With an electric mixer, beat the egg whites until foamy. Sift over the cream of tartar and salt and continue to beat until the whites hold soft peaks when the beaters are lifted.

**4** ▲ Add the remaining sugar in 3 batches, beating well after each addition. Stir in the vanilla and almond essences.

**5** ▲ Add the flour mixture, in 2 batches, and fold in with a large metal spoon after each addition.

**6** Transfer to an ungreased 10 in (25 cm) tube tin and bake until just browned on top, about 1 hour.

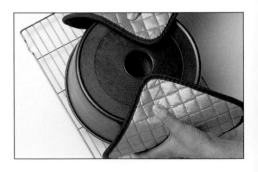

**7** ▲ Turn the tin upside down onto a cake rack and let cool for 1 hour. If the cake does not turn out, run a knife around the edge to loosen it. Invert on a serving plate.

**8** When cool, lay a star-shaped template on top of the cake, sift over icing sugar and remove template.

# Spice Cake with Cream Cheese Frosting

**SERVES 10–12**

| |
|---|
| 10 fl oz (300 ml) milk |
| 2 tablespoons golden syrup |
| 2 teaspoons vanilla essence |
| 3 oz (85 g) walnuts, chopped |
| 6 oz (170 g) butter, at room temperature |
| 10¹/₂ oz (300 g) sugar |
| 1 egg, at room temperature |
| 3 egg yolks, at room temperature |
| 10 oz (285 g) plain flour |
| 1 tablespoon baking powder |
| 1 teaspoon grated nutmeg |
| 1 teaspoon ground cinnamon |
| ¹/₂ teaspoon ground cloves |
| ¹/₄ teaspoon ground ginger |
| ¹/₄ teaspoon ground allspice |
| FOR THE FROSTING |
| 6 oz (170 g) cream cheese |
| 1 oz (30 g) unsalted butter |
| 70 oz (200 g) icing sugar |
| 2 tablespoons finely chopped stem ginger |
| 2 tablespoons syrup from stem ginger |
| stem ginger pieces, for decorating |

**1** Preheat a 350°F/180°C/Gas 4 oven. Line 3 8 in (20 cm) cake tins with greaseproof paper and grease. In a bowl, combine the milk, golden syrup, vanilla and walnuts.

**2** ▼ With an electric mixer, cream the butter and sugar until light and fluffy. Beat in the egg and egg yolks. Add the milk mixture and stir well.

**3** Sift together the flour, baking powder and spices 3 times.

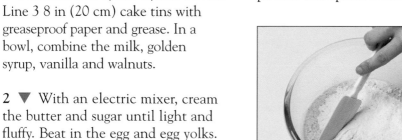

**4** ▲ Add the flour mixture in 4 batches, and fold in carefully after each addition.

**5** Divide the cake mixture between the tins. Bake until the cakes spring back when touched lightly, about 25 minutes. Let stand 5 minutes, then turn out and cool on a rack.

**6** ▼ For the frosting, combine all the ingredients and beat with an electric mixer. Spread the frosting between the layers and over the top. Decorate with pieces of stem ginger.

# Caramel Layer Cake

**SERVES 8–10**

10 oz (285 g) plain flour

1½ teaspoons baking powder

6 oz (170 g) butter, at room
temperature

5½ oz (150 g) caster sugar

4 eggs, at room temperature, beaten

1 teaspoon vanilla essence

8 tablespoons milk

whipped cream, for decorating

caramel threads, for decorating
(optional, see below)

FOR THE FROSTING

10½ oz (300 g) dark brown sugar

8 fl oz (250 ml) milk

1 oz (30 g) unsalted butter

3–5 tablespoons whipping cream

**1** Preheat a 350°F/180°C/Gas 4 oven.
Line 2 8 in (20 cm) cake tins with
greaseproof paper and grease lightly.

**2** ▲ Sift the flour and baking powder
together 3 times. Set aside.

~ COOK'S TIP ~

To make caramel threads, combine
2½ oz (70 g) sugar and 2 fl oz (65 ml)
water in a heavy saucepan. Boil until
light brown. Dip the pan in cold water
to halt cooking. Trail from a spoon on
an oiled baking sheet.

**3** With an electric mixer, cream the
butter and caster sugar until light
and fluffy.

**4** ▲ Slowly mix in the beaten eggs.
Add the vanilla. Fold in the flour
mixture, alternating with the milk.

**5** ▲ Divide the batter between the
prepared tins and spread evenly,
hollowing out the centres slightly.

**6** Bake until the cakes pull away from
the sides of the tin, about 30 minutes.
Let stand 5 minutes, then turn out
and cool on a rack.

**7** ▲ For the frosting, combine the
brown sugar and milk in a saucepan.

**8** Bring to the boil, cover and cook
for 3 minutes. Remove lid and
continue to boil, without stirring, until
the mixture reaches 238°F/119°C (soft
ball stage) on a sugar thermometer.

**9** ▲ Immediately remove the pan
from the heat and add the butter, but
do not stir it in. Let cool until
lukewarm, then beat until the mixture
is smooth and creamy.

**10** Stir in enough cream to obtain a
spreadable consistency. If necessary,
refrigerate to thicken more.

**11** ▲ Spread a layer of frosting on
top of one cake. Sandwich with the
second cake, then spread the top and
sides with the rest of the frosting and
smooth the surface.

**12** To decorate, pipe whipped cream
rosettes around the edge. If using,
place a mound of caramel threads in
the centre before serving.

# Raspberry-Hazelnut Meringue Cake

**SERVES 8**

| |
|---|
| 5 oz (140 g) hazelnuts |
| 4 egg whites |
| ¹/₈ teaspoon salt |
| 7 oz (200 g) sugar |
| ¹/₂ teaspoon vanilla essence |
| FOR THE FILLING |
| 10 fl oz (300 ml) whipping cream |
| 1 lb 8 oz (700 g) raspberries |

**1** Preheat a 350°F/180°C/Gas 4 oven. Line the bottom of 2 8 in (20 cm) cake tins with greaseproof paper and grease.

**2** Spread the hazelnuts on a baking sheet and bake until lightly toasted, about 8 minutes. Let cool slightly.

**3** ▲ Rub the hazelnuts vigorously in a clean tea towel to remove most of the skins.

**4** Grind the nuts in a food processor, blender, or coffee grinder until they are the consistency of coarse sand.

**5** Reduce oven to 300°F/150°C/Gas 2.

**6** With an electric mixer, beat the egg whites and salt until they hold stiff peaks. Beat in 2 tablespoons of the sugar, then fold in the remaining sugar, a few tablespoons at a time, with a rubber scraper. Fold in the vanilla and the hazelnuts.

**7** ▲ Divide the batter between the prepared tins and spread level.

**8** Bake for 1¹/₄ hours. If the meringues brown too quickly, protect with a sheet of foil. Let stand 5 minutes, then carefully run a knife around the inside edge of the tins to loosen. Turn out onto a rack to cool.

**9** For the filling, whip the cream just until firm.

**10** ▲ Spread half the cream in an even layer on one meringue round and top with half the raspberries.

**11** Top with the other meringue round. Spread the remaining cream on top and arrange the remaining raspberries over the cream. Refrigerate for 1 hour to facilitate cutting.

# Forgotten Gâteau

**SERVES 6**

6 egg whites, at room temperature

$^1/_2$ teaspoon cream of tartar

$^1/_8$ teaspoon salt

$10^1/_2$ oz (300 g) caster sugar

1 teaspoon vanilla essence

6 fl oz (175 ml) whipping cream

FOR THE SAUCE

12 oz (350 g) fresh or thawed frozen
raspberries

2–3 tablespoons icing sugar

**1** Preheat a 450°F/230°C/Gas 8 oven.
Grease a $2^1/_3$ pt (1.5 litre) ring mould.

**2** ▲ With an electric mixer, beat the
egg whites, cream of tartar and salt
until they hold soft peaks. Gradually
add the sugar and beat until glossy and
stiff. Fold in the vanilla.

**3** ▲ Spoon into the prepared mould
and smooth the top level.

**4** Place in the oven, then turn the
oven off. Leave overnight; do not
open the oven door at any time.

**5** ▼ To serve, gently loosen the edge
with a sharp knife and turn out onto a
serving plate. Whip the cream until
firm. Spread it over the top and upper
sides of the meringue and decorate
with any meringue crumbs.

**6** ▲ For the sauce, purée the fruit,
then strain. Sweeten to taste.

~ COOK'S TIP ~

This recipe is not suitable for fan
assisted and solid fuel ovens.

# Lemon Coconut Layer Cake

**SERVES 8–10**

| |
|---|
| 6 oz (175 g) plain flour |
| 1/4 teaspoon salt |
| 7 eggs |
| 12 oz (350 g) caster sugar |
| 1 tablespoon grated orange rind |
| grated rind of 1 1/2 lemons |
| juice of 1 lemon |
| 2 1/2 oz (65 g) desiccated coconut |
| 1 tablespoon cornflour |
| 4 fl oz (120 ml) water |
| 1 1/2 oz (40 g) butter |
| FOR THE FROSTING |
| 3 oz (75 g) unsalted butter |
| 6 oz (175 g) icing sugar |
| grated rind of 1 1/2 lemon |
| 2 tablespoons lemon juice |
| 7 oz (200 g) desiccated coconut |

**1** Preheat the oven to 350°F/180°C/ Gas 4. Line three 8 in (20 cm) cake tins with greaseproof paper and grease. In a bowl, sift together the flour and salt and set aside.

**2** ▲ Place six of the eggs in a large heatproof bowl set over hot water. With an electric mixer, beat until frothy. Gradually beat in 8 oz (225 g) caster sugar until the mixture doubles in volume and leaves a ribbon trail when the beaters are lifted, about 10 minutes.

**3** ▲ Remove the bowl from the hot water. Fold in the orange rind, half the grated lemon rind and 1 tablespoon of the lemon juice until blended. Fold in the coconut.

**4** Sift over the flour mixture in three batches, gently folding in thoroughly after each addition.

**5** ▲ Divide the mixture between the prepared tins.

**6** Bake until the cakes pull away from the sides of the tins, 20–25 minutes. Leave to stand for 5 minutes, then turn out to cool on a rack.

**7** In a bowl, blend the cornflour with a little cold water to dissolve. Whisk in the remaining egg just until blended. Set aside.

**8** ▲ In a saucepan, combine the remaining lemon rind and juice, the water, remaining sugar and butter.

**9** Over a medium heat, bring the mixture to the boil. Whisk in the eggs and cornflour mixture, and return to the boil. Whisk continuously until thick, about 5 minutes. Remove from the heat and pour into a bowl. Cover with clear film and set aside to cool.

**10** ▲ For the frosting, cream the butter and icing sugar until smooth. Stir in the lemon rind and enough lemon juice to obtain a thick, spreadable consistency.

**11** Sandwich the three cake layers with the lemon custard mixture. Spread the frosting over the top and sides. Cover the cake with the coconut, pressing it in gently.

# Lemon Yogurt Ring

**SERVES 12**

8 oz (225 g) butter, at room temperature

10½ oz (300 g) caster sugar

4 eggs, at room temperature, separated

2 teaspoons grated lemon rind

3 fl oz (85 ml) lemon juice

8 fl oz (250 ml) plain yogurt

10 oz (285 g) plain flour

2 teaspoons baking powder

1 teaspoon bicarbonate of soda

½ teaspoon salt

FOR THE GLAZE

4 oz (115 g) icing sugar

2 tablespoons lemon juice

3–4 tablespoons plain yogurt

**1** Preheat a 350°F/180°C/Gas 4 oven. Grease a 4⅔ pt (3 litre) bundt or fluted tube tin and dust with flour.

**2** With an electric mixer, cream the butter and caster sugar until light and fluffy. Add the egg yolks, 1 at a time, beating well after each addition.

**3** ▲ Add the lemon rind, juice and yogurt and stir to blend.

**4** Sift together the flour, baking powder and bicarbonate of soda. In another bowl, beat the egg whites and salt until they hold stiff peaks.

**5** ▲ Fold the dry ingredients into the butter mixture, then fold in a dollop of egg whites. Fold in the remaining whites until blended.

**6** Pour into the tin and bake until a skewer inserted in the centre comes out clean, about 50 minutes. Let stand 15 minutes, then turn out and cool on a rack.

**7** For the glaze, sift the icing sugar into a bowl. Stir in the lemon juice and just enough yogurt to make a smooth glaze.

**8** ▲ Set the cooled cake on the rack over a sheet of greaseproof paper or a baking sheet. Pour over the glaze and let it drip down the sides. Allow the glaze to set before serving.

# Soured Cream Crumble Cake

**SERVES 12–14**

| |
|---|
| 4 oz (115 g) butter, at room temperature |
| 4¹/₂ oz (125 g) caster sugar |
| 3 eggs, at room temperature |
| 7¹/₂ oz (215 g) plain flour |
| 1 teaspoon bicarbonate of soda |
| 1 teaspoon baking powder |
| 8 fl oz (250 ml) soured cream |
| FOR THE TOPPING |
| 8 oz (225 g) dark brown sugar |
| 2 teaspoons ground cinnamon |
| 4 oz (115 g) walnuts, finely chopped |
| 2 oz (55 g) cold butter, cut into pieces |

**1** Preheat a 350°F/180°C/Gas 4 oven. Line the bottom of a 9 in (23 cm) square cake tin with greaseproof paper and grease.

**2** ▲ For the topping, place the brown sugar, cinnamon and walnuts in a bowl. Mix with your fingertips, then add the butter and continue working with your fingertips until the mixture resembles breadcrumbs.

**3** To make the cake, cream the butter with an electric mixer until soft. Add the sugar and continue beating until the mixture is light and fluffy.

**4** Add the eggs, 1 at a time, beating well after each addition.

**5** In another bowl, sift the flour, bicarbonate of soda and baking powder together 3 times.

**6** ▲ Fold the dry ingredients into the butter mixture in 3 batches, alternating with the soured cream. Fold until blended after each addition.

**7** ▲ Pour half of the batter into the prepared tin and sprinkle over half of the walnut crumb topping mixture.

**8** Pour the remaining batter on top and sprinkle over the remaining walnut crumb mixture.

**9** Bake until browned, 60–70 minutes. Let stand 5 minutes, then turn out and cool on a rack.

# Sachertorte

**SERVES 8–10**

| |
|---|
| 4 oz (115 g) plain chocolate |
| 3 oz (85 g) unsalted butter, at room temperature |
| 2 oz (55 g) sugar |
| 4 eggs, separated |
| 1 extra egg white |
| 1/4 teaspoon salt |
| 2 1/2 oz (70 g) plain flour, sifted |
| FOR THE TOPPING |
| 5 tablespoons apricot jam |
| 8 fl oz (250 ml) plus 1 tablespoon water |
| 1/2 oz (15 g) unsalted butter |
| 6 oz (170 g) plain chocolate |
| 3 oz (85 g) sugar |
| ready-made chocolate decorating icing (optional) |

**1** Preheat the oven to 325°F/170°C/ Gas 3. Line a 9 × 2 in (23 × 5 cm) cake tin with greaseproof paper and grease.

**2** ▲ Melt the chocolate in the top of a double boiler, or in a heatproof bowl set over hot water. Set aside.

**3** With an electric mixer, cream the butter and sugar until light and fluffy. Stir in the chocolate.

**4** ▲ Beat in the yolks, 1 at a time.

**5** In another bowl, beat the egg whites with the salt until stiff.

**6** ▲ Fold a dollop of whites into the chocolate mixture to lighten it. Fold in the remaining whites in 3 batches, alternating with the sifted flour.

**7** ▲ Pour into the tin and bake until a cake tester comes out clean, about 45 minutes. Turn out onto a rack.

**8** ▲ Meanwhile, melt the jam with 1 tablespoon of the water over low heat, then strain for a smooth consistency.

**9** For the frosting, melt the butter and chocolate in the top of a double boiler or a bowl set over hot water.

**10** ▲ In a heavy saucepan, dissolve the sugar in the remaining water over low heat. Raise the heat and boil until it reaches 225°F/107°C (thread stage) on a sugar thermometer. Immediately plunge the bottom of the pan into cold water for 1 minute. Pour into the chocolate mixture and stir to blend. Let cool for a few minutes.

**11** To assemble, brush the warm jam over the cake. Starting in the centre, pour over the frosting and work outward in a circular movement. Tilt the rack to spread; use a palette knife to smooth the side of the cake. Leave to set overnight. If wished, decorate with chocolate icing.

# Chocolate Frosted Layer Cake

**SERVES 8**

| |
|---|
| 8 oz (225 g) butter or margarine, at room temperature |
| 10¹/₂ oz (300 g) sugar |
| 4 eggs, at room temperature, separated |
| 2 teaspoons vanilla essence |
| 13¹/₂ oz (385 g) plain flour |
| 2 teaspoons baking powder |
| ¹/₈ teaspoon salt |
| 8 fl oz (250 ml) milk |
| FOR THE FROSTING |
| 5 oz (140 g) plain chocolate |
| 4 fl oz (125 ml) soured cream |
| ¹/₈ teaspoon salt |

**1** Preheat a 350°F/180°C/Gas 4 oven. Line 2 8 in (20 cm) round cake tins with greaseproof paper and grease. Dust the tins with flour and shake to evenly distribute. Tap to dislodge excess flour.

**2** With an electric mixer, cream the butter or margarine until soft. Gradually add the sugar and continue beating until light and fluffy.

**3** ▲ Lightly beat the egg yolks, then mix into the creamed butter and sugar with the vanilla.

**4** Sift the flour with the baking powder 3 times. Set aside.

**5** In another bowl, beat the egg whites with the salt until they hold stiff peaks. Set aside.

**6** ▲ Gently fold the dry ingredients into the butter mixture in 3 batches, alternating with the milk.

**7** Add a large dollop of the whites and fold in to lighten the mixture. Carefully fold in the remaining whites until just blended.

**8** Divide the batter between the tins and bake until the cakes pull away from the sides of the tins, about 30 minutes. Let stand 5 minutes. Turn out and cool on a rack.

**9** ▲ For the frosting, melt the chocolate in the top of a double boiler or a bowl set over hot water. When cool, stir in the soured cream and salt.

**10** Sandwich the layers with frosting, then spread on the top and side.

# Devil's Food Cake with Orange Frosting

**SERVES 8–10**

| |
|---|
| 2 oz (55 g) unsweetened cocoa powder |
| 6 fl oz (175 ml) boiling water |
| 6 oz (170 g) butter, at room temperature |
| 12 oz (350 g) dark brown sugar |
| 3 eggs, at room temperature |
| 10 oz (285 g) plain flour |
| 1½ teaspoons bicarbonate of soda |
| ¼ teaspoon baking powder |
| 4 fl oz (125 ml) soured cream |
| orange rind strips, for decoration |

FOR THE FROSTING

| |
|---|
| 10½ oz (300 g) caster sugar |
| 2 egg whites |
| 4 tablespoons frozen orange juice concentrate |
| 1 tablespoon lemon juice |
| grated rind of 1 orange |

**1** Preheat a 350°F/180°C/Gas 4 oven. Line 2 9 in (23 cm) cake tins with greaseproof paper and grease. In a bowl, mix the cocoa and water until smooth. Set aside.

**2** With an electric mixer, cream the butter and sugar until light and fluffy. Add the eggs, 1 at a time, beating well after each addition.

**3** ▲ When the cocoa mixture is lukewarm, add to the butter mixture.

**4** ▼ Sift together the flour, soda and baking powder twice. Fold into the cocoa mixture in 3 batches, alternating with the soured cream.

**5** Pour into the tins and bake until the cakes pull away from the sides of the tins, 30–35 minutes. Let stand 15 minutes. Turn out onto a rack.

**6** Thinly slice the orange rind strips. Blanch in boiling water for 1 minute.

**7** ▲ For the frosting, place all the ingredients in the top of a double boiler or in a bowl set over hot water. With an electric mixer, beat until the mixture holds soft peaks. Continue beating off the heat until thick enough to spread.

**8** Sandwich the cake layers with frosting, then spread over the top and side. Arrange the blanched orange rind strips on top of the cake.

# Walnut Coffee Gâteau

**SERVES 8–10**

| |
|---|
| 5 oz (140 g) walnuts |
| 5¹/₂ oz (150 g) sugar |
| 5 eggs, separated |
| 2 oz (55 g) dry breadcrumbs |
| 1 tablespoon unsweetened cocoa powder |
| 1 tablespoon instant coffee |
| 2 tablespoons rum or lemon juice |
| ¹/₈ teaspoon salt |
| 6 tablespoons redcurrant jelly |
| chopped walnuts, for decorating |
| FOR THE FROSTING |
| 8 oz (225 g) plain chocolate |
| 1¹/₄ pt (750 ml) whipping cream |

**1** ▲ For the frosting, combine the chocolate and cream in the top of a double boiler, or in a heatproof bowl set over simmering water. Stir until the chocolate melts. Let cool, then cover and refrigerate overnight or until the mixture is firm.

**2** Preheat the oven to 350°F/180°C/ Gas 4. Line a 9 × 2 in (23 × 5 cm) cake tin with greaseproof paper and grease.

**3** ▲ Grind the nuts with 3 tablespoons of the sugar in a food processor, blender, or coffee grinder.

**4** With an electric mixer, beat the egg yolks and remaining sugar until thick and lemon-coloured.

**5** ▲ Fold in the walnuts. Stir in the breadcrumbs, cocoa, coffee and rum or lemon juice.

**6** ▲ In another bowl, beat the egg whites with the salt until they hold stiff peaks. Fold carefully into the walnut mixture with a rubber scraper.

**7** Pour the meringue batter into the prepared tin and bake until the top of the cake springs back when touched lightly, about 45 minutes. Let the cake stand for 5 minutes, then turn out and cool on a rack.

**8** ▲ When cool, slice the cake in half horizontally.

**9** With an electric mixer, beat the chocolate frosting mixture on low speed until it becomes lighter, about 30 seconds. Do not overbeat or it may become grainy.

**10** ▲ Warm the jelly in a saucepan until melted, then brush over the cut cake layer. Spread with some of the chocolate frosting, then sandwich with the remaining cake layer. Brush the top of the cake with jelly, then cover the side and top with the remaining chocolate frosting. Make a starburst pattern by pressing gently with a table knife in lines radiating from the centre. Sprinkle the chopped walnuts around the edge.

# Classic Cheesecake

**SERVES 8**

2 oz (55 g) digestive biscuits, crushed

2 lb (900 g) cream cheese, at room temperature

8³/₄ oz (240 g) sugar

grated rind of 1 lemon

3 tablespoons lemon juice

1 teapoon vanilla essence

4 eggs, at room temperature

**1** Preheat the oven to 325°F/170°C/ Gas 3. Grease an 8 in (20 cm) springform tin. Place on a round of foil 4–5 in (10–12.5 cm) larger than the diameter of the tin. Press it up the sides to seal tightly.

**2** Sprinkle the crushed biscuits in the base of the tin. Press to form an even layer.

**3** With an electric mixer, beat the cream cheese until smooth. Add the sugar, lemon rind and juice, and vanilla, and beat until blended. Beat in the eggs, 1 at a time. Beat just enough to blend thoroughly.

**4** ▲ Pour into the prepared tin. Set the tin in a larger baking tray and place in the oven. Pour enough hot water in the outer tray to come 1 in (2.5 cm) up the side of the tin.

**5** Bake until the top of the cake is golden brown, about 1¹/₂ hours. Let cool in the tin.

**6** ▼ Run a knife around the edge to loosen, then remove the rim of the tin. Refrigerate for at least 4 hours before serving.

# Chocolate Cheesecake

**SERVES 10–12**

10 oz (285 g) plain chocolate

2 lb 8 oz (1.2 kg) cream cheese, at room temperature

7 oz (200 g) sugar

2 teaspoons vanilla essence

4 eggs, at room temperature

6 fl oz (175 ml) soured cream

1 tablespoon cocoa powder

FOR THE BASE

7 oz (200 g) chocolate biscuits, crushed

3 oz (85 g) butter, melted

¹/₂ teaspoon ground cinnamon

**1** Preheat a 350°F/180°C/Gas 4 oven. Grease the bottom and sides of a 9 × 3 in (23 × 7.5 cm) springform tin.

**2** ▲ For the base, mix the crushed biscuits with the butter and cinnamon. Press evenly onto the bottom of the tin.

**3** Melt the chocolate in the top of a double boiler, or in a heatproof bowl set over hot water. Set aside.

**4** Beat the cream cheese until smooth, then beat in the sugar and vanilla. Add the eggs, 1 at a time.

**5** Stir the soured cream into the cocoa powder to form a paste. Add to the cream cheese mixture. Stir in the melted chocolate.

**6** ▼ Pour into the crust. Bake for 1 hour. Let cool in the tin; remove rim. Refrigerate before serving.

*Classic Cheesecake (top), Chocolate Cheesecake*

# Marbled Cheesecake

**SERVES 10**

| |
|---|
| 2 oz (55 g) unsweetened cocoa powder |
| 5 tablespoons hot water |
| 2 lb (900 g) cream cheese, at room temperature |
| 7 oz (200 g) sugar |
| 4 eggs |
| 1 teaspoon vanilla essence |
| 2¹/₂ oz (70 g) digestive biscuits, crushed |

**1** Preheat a 350°F/180°C/Gas 4 oven. Line an 8 × 3 in (20 × 8 cm) cake tin with greaseproof paper and grease.

**2** Sift the cocoa powder into a bowl. Pour over the hot water and stir to dissolve. Set aside.

**3** With an electric mixer, beat the cheese until smooth and creamy. Add the sugar and beat to incorporate. Beat in the eggs, one at a time. Do not overmix.

**4** Divide the mixture evenly between 2 bowls. Stir the chocolate mixture into one, then add the vanilla to the remaining mixture.

**5** ▲ Pour a cupful of the plain mixture into the centre of the tin; it will spread out into an even layer. Slowly pour over a cupful of chocolate mixture in the centre.

**6** ▲ Repeat alternating cupfuls of the batters in a circular pattern until both are used up.

**7** Set the tin in a larger baking tray and pour in hot water to come 1¹/₂ in (3 cm) up the sides of the cake tin.

**8** Bake until the top of the cake is golden, about 1¹/₂ hours. It will rise during baking but will sink later. Let cool in the tin on a rack.

**9** To turn out, run a knife around the inside edge. Place a flat plate, bottom-side up, over the tin and invert onto the plate.

**10** ▼ Sprinkle the crushed biscuits evenly over the base, gently place another plate over them, and invert again. Cover and refrigerate for at least 3 hours, or overnight. To serve, cut slices with a sharp knife dipped in hot water.

# Index